To Christine
    May the Peace of Christ alwa

THE
PEOPLE
of
TRINITY PRESBYTERIAN CHURCH
OMAGH

Moderator
Presbyterian Church in Ireland
    30 Sept 04

1754-2004

Claire McElhinney   30/9/04

John McCandless.

John McCandless
Claire McElhinney

Published by Trinity Presbyterian Church, Omagh

Editorial advisers:
Rev Robert Herron
Margaret Simms

Digital Image Photography
Kenneth Allen

Contributors
R A Elliott
Mavis Jardine
Ian Leitch
Hazel McCay
Marie Neary
Heather Watson

Researchers
Derek Duffield
Alex Elder
Sammy Gallagher
Irene Knox
Audrey McConnell
Jeanette Millar
Ronnie Orr

Published by Trinity Presbyterian Church, Omagh
c/o Glenart
12 Knocksilla Park
Omagh
Co Tyrone
BT79 OAR

September 2004

ISBN   0-9548141-0-X *Softback*   0-9548141-1-8 *Hardback*

This publication has been supported by the Ulster Local History Trust

Printed by The Universities Press, Belfast

Front cover photograph by Kenneth Allen
Trinity Presbyterian Church, Hall and Sexton's House from James Street, Omagh (February 2004)

CONTENTS

FOREWORD

T he 250th birthday of any organisation is a reasonable excuse for celebration. I am delighted that the Church Committee of Trinity has chosen to use the occasion as an opportunity to put on record all that could be determined about its history. Trinity Presbyterian Church in Omagh remains on its original site and we are pleased to be part of a little community of churches that stand together on the elevated land above and beyond the Courthouse.

Although this book is about Trinity Church and its people, I congratulate the authors, Claire and John, for the way they have managed to blend together details about the development of Trinity with the parallel development of Omagh as an important county town. The people of Trinity were townspeople of Omagh and it is clear that, down the years, those people made significant contributions to the town's commercial and civic life. The personal profiles in the pages of the book reflect their strength of character and their Christian outlook.

This book has taken several years to produce and has involved a lot of effort by a large team of helpers. On behalf of the congregation I take this opportunity to formally thank all who contributed in any way. I believe that the material produced is testament to the quality of their efforts.

Local history is a rich tapestry of past times that includes documents, records, historic buildings, photographs and the remembered customs, practices and sayings of the people of the times. Most of all local history is for sharing. It is my hope that all who read this book will enjoy the experience as well as appreciating more about our church's history and that of its mother town.

Robert Herron

INTRODUCTION

SECOND Omagh Presbyterian Church (now Trinity) is the oldest Church on its existing site in Omagh. Opened in 1754, it has been in existence since before America's independence was declared in 1776 and its subsequent separation from England in 1782. It has stood through the times of the great French Revolution, the wars of Napoleon, the British victories at land and sea under Wellington and Nelson, the Crimea and Boer wars and the reigns of 10 British monarchs. In Ireland it has seen the rebellion of 1798, Emmet's insurrection in 1801 and the establishment of the Irish Free State in 1921.

This book traces the history of Trinity Presbyterian Church, Omagh and its people since the site was purchased in 1752 to the present time. It outlines the reason behind the establishment of the Church and attempts to place this in the context of the development of Presbyterianism in Ireland and, more specifically, the Omagh area. It highlights the key stages in the development of the Church which was, until 1910, known as Second Omagh Presbyterian Church. The book gives profiles of members of the congregations through the years and highlights their positions, influence and contributions in the wider Omagh communities where they lived and worked. The Church's progress is framed against similar Church developments in the Omagh area and other significant national and international events. The diverse nature and make-up of the congregation is examined, revealing a continual change in personnel and families through time and the impact that such change has had.

According to Church records, the first meeting-house became dilapidated in appearance in 1855 and it was demolished and rebuilt. The new church had a gallery and was heated by two fireplaces and two stoves. There was no musical instrument in the new Church , and the choir, who sang a limited number of Psalms, sat in the gallery above and behind most of the congregation. Lighting was by candles and oil lamps, which were succeeded by gas and later, in the 1930s, by electricity.

A major extension in 1901 saw the removal of the gallery, the addition of two transepts, a new entrance porch at the front and a Minister's room and two new entrance doors at the rear. The church building today is little changed from that time.

Finally the impact of the Northern Ireland 'troubles' and the Omagh bomb is considered from the viewpoint of ordinary Presbyterians in a local community.

The Establishment of Second Omagh Congregation

ACONGREGATION of Presbyterians had been active in Omagh from around 1656. By the year 1673, when an over-worked cleric, Rev John Rowatt, was ministering to several Churches in the area, his plight was debated by the Presbytery of Letterkenny (to which Omagh belonged). It was decided that he would be relieved of some of his parishes in order to minister "every third Lord's Day in Drumraar." The Presbytery recommended the provision of a new meeting-house. It also directed that the "meeting-house must be built in or near the Omey." It is thought that this Church was situated in the Crevenagh area. (A fuller but quite brief history of the early development of Presbyterianism in Ireland and thence in Omagh is included at Appendices 1 and 2.)

In 1699 **Rev James Maxwell** was called to the meeting-house in Omagh. Before his ordination he had to attain a satisfactory standard in Classics, so he delivered an exegesis in Latin, preached a sermon on Psalm 89, v 15, was able to read any part of the New Testament in Greek and passed an examination in Hebrew! He was promised a stipend of £40 a year in cash and also 40 barrels of oats. Before his services began he stipulated that neither the Presbytery "nor the people, might expect from him so frequent family visits as are usual in other places where the bounds are less." So Mr Maxwell began his ministry in Omagh and when the congregation was firmly established, a new meeting-house for Omagh was built on the Dublin Road in 1721. It was a barn church built in a T shape. It accommodated about 800, many of whom did not sit but stood throughout the service. That church building was more recently (twentieth century) used by Montgomery's printing works.

This Presbyterian Meeting-house at Dublin Road, Omagh served as the church for all Presbyterians in the town prior to 1752. The original building has been preserved and reconstructed at the Ulster Folk and Transport Museum.

An artist's impression of Omagh Meeting-house (1721) at Dublin Road showing the traditional T shape of the building.

Some time during the ministry of Mr Maxwell the Longfield or Drumquin part of his congregation was separated from Omagh and was attached to the newly formed congregation of Castlederg, but the exact date of its separation is uncertain.

On 4 May 1742, when Omagh consisted of between 50 and 60 thatch-covered houses, the town was almost entirely destroyed by an accidental fire, caused by a servant throwing out ashes near a hay-stack behind her master's house. Only a few buildings with tiled roofs escaped, including the Presbyterian Meeting-house, the Parish Church, the Gaol, the Courthouse and a few private residences. Shortly afterwards the Synod of Ulster met at Dungannon and an appeal from the townspeople for assistance was granted.

On 1 February 1750 Rev Maxwell died at the age of 89, having served the Presbyterians of Omagh for more than 50 years. Until then the town's Presbyterians were united in the one Church at Dublin Road.

When he died on 1 February 1750 Rev Maxwell left a son, John, who was ordained Minister of Armagh in 1732, and a daughter, who became the wife of Rev Andrew Welsh, Minister of Ardstraw. Numerous descendants included the Rodgers families of Cavanacaw and Edergole, the Booth family of Denamona and the Clements and Galbraith families. Thomas Rodger of Edergole was soon to play an important role in the establishment of a second Presbyterian congregation in Omagh.

On 5 June 1751 **Rev Hugh Delap** was ordained to succeed Mr Maxwell, but his election was not unanimous and this led to a minority of 50 families separating from the Church, under the leadership of Messrs William Scott and James Nixon. At a meeting of the General Synod at Dungannon on 16 June 1752 these leaders presented a supplication stating that they never had subjected themselves to Mr Delap's ministry, nor would they do it, and desired that they might be erected into a separate Worshipping Congregation, proposing to give undeniable security for the comfortable support of a Minister. This was opposed by Mr John Buchanan, on behalf of Mr Delap's congregation, who argued that the request should not be met and, if granted, would be "attended with very bad consequences." However, the application was granted and they were annexed to the Presbytery of Strabane. The remaining Church was initially referred to as the "Old Meeting-house". The old Meeting-house was then named "First Omagh". The separated families built the "New Meeting-house", later to be known as "Second Omagh" and, more recently still, "Trinity Presbyterian Church".

It was on 17 July 1752 that "John Scott of Strathroi, Thos Rodger of Edergole, David Campbell of Omagh and William McConnell of Tattyneur" lent their names to the following Indendure to purchase land to build a 'meeting-house'. This land remains the site on which Trinity Presbyterian Church, Omagh stands today. The purchase document is the earliest official record of its history held by the Church. Its text is reproduced in full on page 9:

THIS INDENTURE made this seventeenth day of July, in the name of our Lord God, One Thousand Seven Hundred and Fifty Two BETWEEN Mr ALEXANDER McCAUSLAND of Omagh and County of Tyrone on the one part and JOHN SCOTT of Stroghroy, THOMAS RODGER of Edergole DAVID CAMPBELL of Omagh and WILLIAM McCONNELL of Tattenueir all of said County of the other part witnesseth that the said Alexander McCausland for and in consideration of the rents, covenants, payments and agreements hereafter reserved and contained hath granted, bargained and confirmed and by these presents both grant, bargain and confirm unto the said John Scott, Thomas Rodger, David Campbell and William McConnell, ALL THAT plot of ground near Omagh, County aforesaid as it is now marked out for building a meetinghouse thereon said plot of ground having the lane or road leading to Russ's Park on the north Archibald Kerr's tenements on the east surrounded on the west and south by the parks now in possession of James Maxwell to have and to hold the said plot of ground above mentioned from the first day of November, next ensuing One Thousand Seven Hundred and Fifty Two to the said John Scott, Thomas Rodger, David Campbell and William McConnell their heirs, executors admirations and assignees forever for the proper use of the new erected dissenting congregation of Omagh YIELDING AND PAYING therefor and thereout unto the said Alexander McCausland his heirs or assignees, the sum of thirty shillings sterling yearly and every year forever at the two usual days of payment in the year that is to say on the First day of May and the First day of November by even and equal portions over and above all parliament taxes, subsidies and other country charges whatsoever, and if it shall happen that the said yearly rent or any part or parcell thereof to be behind and unpaid by the space of 20 days next after any of the said days of payment that then it shall and may be lawful to and for the said Alexander McCausland, his heirs or assigns into the premises to enter and distrain and the distress or distresses then and there found to lead, drive and carry away and the same to dispose of according to law and if it shall happen that no sufficient distress or distresses can be had in or upon the premises then it shall and may be lawful to and for the said Alexander McCausland, his heirs or assigns into the premises to re-enter and the same with the appurtenances wholly to have again repossess and re-enjoy untile the said rent and arrears of rent be fully satisfied and paid and the said John Scott, Thomas Rodger, David Campbell and William McConnell for themselves their heirs and assigns both covenant and agree to and with the said Alexander McCausland, to truly observe, perform, fulfil and keep all and every covenants, articles, payments and agreements in these presents mentioned specified and contained with on their parts ought to be paid and done observed, performed, fulfilled and kept upon pain of forfeiting this present Indenture any thing herein to the contrary notwithstanding and the said Alex McCauland both for himself his heirs executors administrators and assigns shall and will at any time hereafter at the reasonable request and at the proper Court and charges of the said John Scott, Thomas Rodger, David Campbell and William McConnell their heirs executors and assigns make and perform execute suffer and do cause to be executed suffered and done unto the said John Scott, Thomas Rodger, David Campbell and William McConnell their heirs executors administrators and assigns all and every such further appearance and assurance which by the learned Councillor in the law of the said John Scott, Thomas Rodger, David Campbell and William McConnell their heirs executors administrators and assigns shall be reasonably devised advised or required for the further confirming and assuring of the said premises and every part thereof unto the said John Scott, Thomas Rodger, David Campbell and William McConnell their heirs onto the use and behalf of the new erected congregation of Omagh working to the true intent and meaning of those presents providing the said Alex McCausland, his heirs, executors administrators and assigns be not compelled to leave from his own house unless at the proper expense of the said John Scott, Thomas Rodger, David Campbell and William McConnell their heirs, executors, administrators and assigns for protecting the same and the said Alex McCausland for himself, his heirs, executors, administrators and assigns both covenant and grant to and with the said John Scott, Thomas Rodger, David Campbell and William McConnell their heirs, executors, administrators and assigns all and singular the bargain presents with the appurtenances and the rents covenants and conditions above recited to serve defend and keep harmless unto the said John Scott, Thomas Rodger, David Campbell and William McConnell, their heirs, executors, administrators or assigns and against all person or persons claiming any title or interest to the bargain presented for and on behalf of the said Alex McCausland.

In witness whereof both parties have interchangeably put their hand and seal the day and year above written.

Signed Sealed and Delivered
in presence of

J.W. Maxwell (signature)   **Alex McCausland (signature)**
John Nixon (signature)

Note that this deed of sale was signed and witnessed by 'J W Maxwell' and 'John Nixon' and a yearly ground rent of 30 shillings per annum was agreed. The land previously belonged to Alex McCausland, who was allowed to live on it unless or until the Church provided for him.

The new Meeting-house, 'Second Omagh', was built at the opposite end of the town, on the Dromore Road, and opened in 1754. This was the first Church to be located in that area, and in the years to follow, other Churches were established there.

In 1777 St Columba's Church of Ireland was built on its present-day site.

The year 1812 saw the Methodist Church built, just opposite Second Omagh and St Columba's. The Methodist Church was rebuilt in 1857.

In 1829 the first Roman Catholic Church was built, in Brook Street. In 1899 it too relocated to its present site at the corner of Church Street and Castle Street.

This completed the cluster of four churches on the same raised ground, which is very much a feature of Omagh today.

Aerial view of churches

Sacred Heart Roman Catholic Church (built 1899)

Omagh Methodist Church (first built 1812)

Trinity Presbyterian Church (first built 1754)

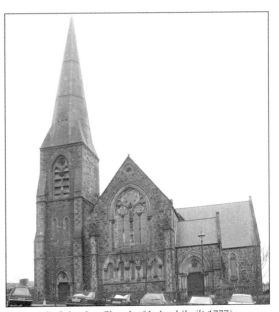

St Columbas Church of Ireland (built 1777)

11

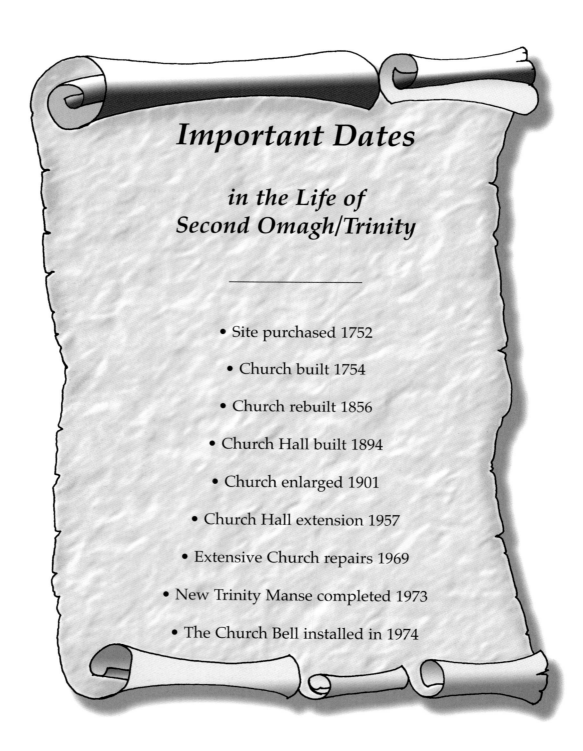

Important Dates

in the Life of
Second Omagh/Trinity

- Site purchased 1752

- Church built 1754

- Church rebuilt 1856

- Church Hall built 1894

- Church enlarged 1901

- Church Hall extension 1957

- Extensive Church repairs 1969

- New Trinity Manse completed 1973

- The Church Bell installed in 1974

The Church Buildings

The first church

The first meeting- house was officially opened in July 1754. It was a traditional Presbyterian building of its time. T-shaped and relatively plain, its design reflected the times when there was only one established Church in Ireland and no state funding for the other Churches. The building did, however, lend its name to the area of Omagh where it stood, and old maps and directories clearly refer to 'Meetinghouse Hill'. This church would have been heated by coal or turf fire and, when necessary, the church interior would have been lighted by candles. The internal layout would have been fairly standard for the time, with the seating focused on the high pulpit which would probably have been in the middle of the longest wall and not on the short wall as is the case today. The congregation would have travelled to church on foot, by horse or in a horse-drawn carriage or trap. Records from this era are scant, but it is recorded that the second meeting-house had no gallery and was 'ceiled' in 1832. It probably also had high-sided pews with doors. The Meeting House at the Ulster American Folk Park is probably quite like the original Second Omagh Church building in both design and layout.

This photo of the eighteenth century Presbyterian meeting-house at the Ulster American Folk Park near Omagh is likely to represent, in approximate appearance, the style of the first Second Omagh Church building.

Until the 1940s this would have been a common mode of transport to Church.

The simplicity of Presbyterian Church architecture in the mid eighteenth century was very similar to the Catholic Churches. The Presbyterians did not want to copy the Gothic style of the Established church and therefore they looked to Scotland for examples which resulted in the 'functional austerity' that is still evident in many Presbyterian buildings today. (Historic Ulster Churches by Simon Walker, p31/2)

Although very little is known about Second Omagh's first Minister, Rev Robert Nelson, it is most likely that he was connected with the many Nelson/Neilsons who became "pastors, educators and Gaelic scholars" in the sixteenth and seventeenth centuries, namely Moses of Rademon, James of Downpatrick and William of Dundalk and Belfast.

Moses Nelson (1739-1823) was born at Craigmonaghan, near Castlederg and married a Catherine Welsh, daughter of Rev Andrew

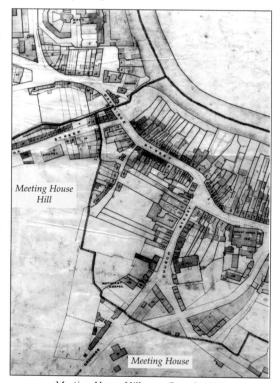

Meeting House Hill area, Omagh 1833

Welsh of Ardstraw. Second Omagh's Minister, Robert Nelson was born in that area about 1730 and from perusal of available information, it is quite possible that he and Moses Nelson were cousins.

Another reference to Rev Nelson's time at Second Omagh is contained in 'a letter of introduction' dated 23 May 1773 that he gave to one of his congregation who emigrated to America. The parishoner in question was a James McGrew and his wife and children. The letter states:

> That James McGrew and wife are Protestant Dissenters of reputable families in this County. That they were members of our congregation. That they are free from all public scandal; that their behaviour has been strictly honest and obliging; that they are entitled to participate of the Privelege of the Christian Church and merit the confidence and encouragement of the virtuous. Attested at Omagh, this 23rd day of May 1773, by Robert Nelson.

This James McGrew emigrated to Charleston, South Carolina and is a direct ancestor of the many McGrew families who still worship in Trinity Church, Omagh.

From the beginning Second Omagh congregation would have elected a Church Committee in accordance with the democratic principles of Presbyterianism. Church Elders would also have been elected at the first opportunity. The Church Committee would meet about once per month, and it is known that this frequency was maintained until 1928, when Rev J Gibson proposed that meetings be held quarterly.

This photograph gives some idea of how Omagh was developing in the late nineteenth century before the arrival of the motor car.

Omagh 1800-1856

In the early nineteenth century Omagh had a population of almost 2,000. Mail was despatched by coach to Dublin at 12.30 pm every day. The coach arrived in Dublin at 6.00 am the following day, when letters for England were despatched onwards. Letters for Scotland were 'diverted' at Aughnacloy, to join up with the Belfast mail and thence across the sea by ferry.

By 1836 there were 2,211 persons in Omagh. They lived in 715 houses, "585 of them respectable and slated". There were paved streets but no lighting. It was at this time that the cost of continual repairs to the church began to give concern, and in the ensuing years a decision was taken in principle to demolish the old church and erect a more modern building on the same site.

The late 1840s and early 1850s were difficult times, coming soon after the impact of the famine in Ireland. There had been a soup-kitchen in Omagh in 1847, and this was followed by several more in other Tyrone towns and villages. At that time Tyrone lost about 60,000 of its population. However, there was a resurgence in Omagh that led to the development of new businesses and the regrowth of the population, which reached 3,485 by 1862.

The Rebuilding of Second Omagh Church

It was some time in 1855 that Rev Josias Mitchell and several senior members of the Church met to progress the earlier decision to rebuild the church. It is recorded that the old church, built in 1752 , was

> in a dilapidated and frail state, especially the roof and pews, and it was not becoming the prominent position which the cause of Presbyterianism is entitled to hold in this rising County town and that it would be better economy to rebuild than to repair the old house.

By this time, application had been made to the Assembly's Building Committee and a grant of £150 received, and "encouraging" subscriptions had also been received from the congregation. An architect, Mr Alexander Hardy, had been employed to draw up plans, and local builder Mr William Scott was awarded the contract to build the new church for the sum of £857. Alexander Hardy was the Church Architect for the Derry Diocese of the Church of Ireland. He was also a brother-in-law of W J McKnight, the Congregational Secretary, and this relationship was probably a major factor in moving ahead with the project at that time. W J McKnight's daughter, Elizabeth, was later to marry T J McAdam, of whom much more will be told later in this publication. The influence of the McKnight family manifested itself once more with the appointment of Rev Robert Wallace as the Church's Minister in 1890. Rev Wallace was W J McKnight's brother-in-law!

It seems clear that the increasing prosperity in the town and the presence and influence of some successful businessmen in Second Omagh congregation were significant factors in driving the major rebuild project. James Greer, a solicitor and wealthy landowner, businessmen John McAdam and John Houston, W J McKnight, Clerk to Omagh Poor Law Union, and several others were the key decision-makers. Indeed, it is quite significant to note how many members of Second Omagh were running successful businesses in the town during the second half of that century and helping to form the backbone of subsequent commercial growth and prosperity . These include Joseph Anderson (later J B Andersons), Henry and Robert Lyons (H and R Lyons), the Houston family (hardware merchants and grocers, 10/12 George's Street), Joseph Wilson (joined Frank Crawford to become Crawford and Wilson), Thomas C Dickie (later Dickie and Carson (solicitors)), John K McConnell (later McConnell and Fyffe (solicitors)), John McAdam (McAdam and Bates), Hugh Kirk and R D Swan (later to become Swan and Mitchell), King Houston (solicitor), John Fallows (monumental sculptor) and William Dale (grocery and hardware business continued by Fred Todd at John Street). Members of the Church were also prominent in civic life as members of the Grand Jury, the Town Commissioners and, later, the Urban and Rural District Councils. In addition, Joseph Anderson, T C Dickie and John K McConnell were founder members of the Omagh YMCA, an organisation that was central to the religious, social and sporting life of Omagh in the first half of the twentieth century.

To progress the rebuild project, the Church Committee met either side of Christmas Day, on 23 and 27 December. It had become obvious that the congregation alone could not raise the required money, so it was decided to follow up all persons who had not yet subscribed and to approach others "in the neighbourhood whom the Committee may think likely to subscribe". In February 1856 a beautifully written letter, signed by J McAdam, Fund Treasurer and W J McKnight, Congregational Secretary (reproduced over), was sent to people who "would be likely to subscribe".

The Congregation worshipping in this Church are at present engaged in an effort to rebuild it. The old Church which has been standing upwards of a century, and which was originally badly constructed, had become very much dilapidated, requiring constant repairs to keep it tenantable. Neither was it so comfortable, nor respectable as a place for the worship of God ought to be. Under these circumstances the Congregation resolved on making an effort to rebuild the house in preference to expending a large sum on repairing it.

They were the more induced to this course, as assistance is available from the Assembly's Building Fund, and from the consideration that if the present opportunity be lost, this fund may in a few years be exhausted, and applied to the erection of Churches in less necessary localities.

Many of the members of the Congregation have contributed largely to this object, and also some friends not belonging to it. But as the expense of erecting a Building worthy of so prominent a position in Ulster, as the Assize Town of County Tyrone, is very considerable, and

and as the congregation is at present comparatively small; and after the utmost exertion on the part of the Members, and also the grant from the Building Fund, a balance of at least £200, will remain; the Committee are obliged to extend their application for aid, beyond the bounds of the Congregation, to such other friends as may approve of so desirable an object.

The Committee desire to enclose you the foregoing statement, and to solicit your kind co-operation and support, and that you will be good enough to bring the subject favorably before such of your friends as might be willing to assist them.

Contributions will be gratefully received by any of the following Members of Committee.

Rev'd Josias Mitchell, James Greer, Esq.
Mess'rs Joseph Macknight, John McAdam, J Houston, W Warnock, W Dudgeon, A McEldowney, S D Mathews, G Gibson, J Buchanan, R Ritter, J Buchanan K Clogher, G Booth, J & E Greer Sol'rs.

J McAdam Treasurer
W J Macknight, Secretary

Omagh,
4th February, 1856.

The "Committee for obtaining subscriptions" was: Rev Josias Mitchell, James Greer Junior, James Scott, John McAdam, John Houston, George Gibson, Edward Greer, John Buchanan (Killyclogher), William J McKnight and John Buchanan (Bonnynubber).

The Building Committee included all members of Church Session and Committee. These were the above-named plus: William Warnock, William Dudgeon, John McCarthy, Andrew McElmurray, Samuel Matthews, James Greer Senior and George Booth. The Committee's first official meeting was on 6 January 1856. The Church solicitors were James and Edward Greer and they were instructed to draw up a Bond of Security between the congregation and William Scott, the builder. (NOTE: The same William Scott had, in 1847, established a business, which was later to become Scott's Excelsior Mills, at Mountjoy Road, Omagh.)

At the next meeting the following matters were agreed:

1   To obtain 100 copies of a lithograph view of the front and side of the new church, the cost not to exceed £1/10/0.

2   To improve the current design of the pews by taking three inches off the length of each side pew and adding this to the length of the centre pews.

3   The centre pews to be divided into two sections.

4   The heating to consist of one stove placed in the vestibule as can be arranged hereafter, with the fireplaces in the pews on either side of the pulpit.

5   Provision to be left in the centre of the House for a stove as first approved.

On the left is a copy of the lithograph obtained by Rev Mitchell in 1856. Remember there were no photographs at that time. A photograph taken c1900 is shown for comparison.

The following extracts taken from the Church minutes help to paint a picture of the progression of this project, the great efforts of the Subscriptions Committee in raising the necessary funds and the generosity of the congregation and community.

> 25 January 1856 The Secretary should write to Rev Arnold of First Omagh Presbyterian Church to extend grateful acknowledgements of this committee for the favour conferred in allowing our congregation to worship in their Church during the rebuilding of our own, and that it is the opinion of this committee that so long as the two congregations worship jointly, the Sabbath collections should be alternatively allocated to the funds of both.

On Friday 7 March 1856 James Greer Junior performed the ceremony of laying the foundation-stone of the new church. A suitable address was delivered on the occasion by the Rev Josias Mitchell to a large and respectable audience. A bottle hermetically sealed was placed under the stone, containing a copy of the minutes of the last Assembly, McComb's Almanac, Irish Presbyterian, Missionary Herald, Banner of Ulster and a parchment with the names of the Elders, Committee and builder.

> 11 April 1856 The builder, William Scott, is looking for payment of the first instalment amounting to £400. It was agreed that £250 would be paid only if 'work to that amount has been satisfactorily executed.' Spouting from the old church would not do the new church, so permission was given to the builder to purchase new spouting. The architect, Mr Hardy, recommended that the finials in the angles of the building and on each side of the entrance door should have an ornamental finial instead of a plain point which would add to the architectural character of the work.

> 19 May 1856 Rev Mitchell suggested that Dr Henry Cooke be invited to preach at the opening of the new church.

> NOTE: It is known that Dr Cooke was a close friend of James Greer Senior.

> 26 June 1856 The cost of the new spouting and finials amounts to £7/10/10, which the builder is to receive from Church funds. The Committee agree that the margin panes of the windows in the new church should be of stained glass and that a new pipe should be brought in for the stove. The margin panes cost £3/9/4.

Every window in the present church has margin panes. That is the coloured strip or line around the margins of the windows. These were an after thought in 1856 and cost a total of £3/9/4.

11 July 1856 A full Committee meeting was held and the architect and builder were also in attendance.

Agreed:

1 The gallery railings should be lowered by 5 inches.
2 Grates with marble shelves should be provided for the fireplaces.
3 For the present, a partition should be put up in the right-hand side of the vestibule for the purpose of forming a small room for the Minister.
4 In the left side of the vestibule under the gallery stairs, a place shall be enclosed for storing coal and turf.
5 The down spouting should be made close to the ground so as to carry the roof water into the sewer which goes round the Church and at the same time prevent the placing of vessels under the spouts.
6 The first Sabbath in September next be fixed for the opening of the new church as Mr Scott expects to have it completed before that day.

The final touches in preparation for the opening included:

1 The appointment of additional collectors.
2 Carpet for the stairs to the pulpit and for the space in front of the pulpit.
3 Matting and mats plus linoleum for the aisles.

It seems remarkable that the entire process of demolishing the old church and designing, planning and building the new one took only nine months. In fact, the church was officially opened exactly six months after the foundation-stone had been laid. This emphasises once again the quality of the people in Second Omagh Church at that time, as well as the great skills of the builders and craftsmen and their capacity for hard work.

Church collections

Acceptance of the invitation to open the church by Rev Dr Henry Cooke was duly received. It is believed that Dr Cooke made it a condition that a charge of one shilling should be made on those attending his sermon but that the proceeds should go to the Building Fund. Admission was therefore by ticket, and the event was advertised in the Derry Standard, the Tyrone Constitution and hand bills. In addition, a collection was to be taken up at both morning and evening services. As was the custom for such special events, collectors were appointed. These were usually very prominent people in the congregation plus invited dignitaries. For the opening of the new church the collectors were: The Hon A G Stuart, Robert D Coulson, Samuel Galbraith, Charles Scott, James Greer, Captain Ellis, George Spiller, Charles Eccles, Samuel King, James Greer Junior, John Buchanan, James F Alexander, Richard Stack and James Meeke. One press report states that "the celebrity of the venerable divine drew together many members of the different Protestant churches of the town and neighbourhood and also some of the Roman Catholic Church."

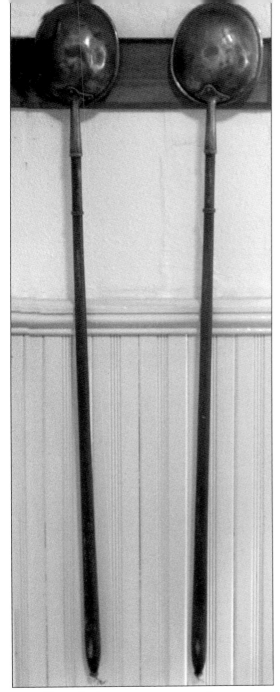

These collecting spoons were common in many churches. The long handle enabled the collector to reach in to everyone in a pew without involving others and perhaps avoiding prying eyes!

The letting of pews

It was the custom in earlier Presbyterian churches that pews were let out, for a fee, to members of the congregation, who would then have their names on a card at each pew. Pews were numbered to facilitate this process, and the letting of pews and fixing of rents was regular business for Committee approval. Up to two families could let each pew, and the higher up the social ladder one was, the better chance one had of obtaining the preferred choice and position of pew. As the new church was nearing completion the Committee resolved that

> the congregation was to be informed on two successive Sundays of the letting of pews and an opportunity afforded them on Tuesday 2 September of attending at the new church and choosing their pews.

Major James Scott, George Gibson and John Buchanan were appointed to assist the Church Secretary, W J McKnight, with pew letting. In cases of disagreement the Committee had the final say. It is also noted that

> in appreciation of the great exertions used by Rev Mitchell and John McAdam in raising subscriptions for and otherwise promoting the erection of the new church, the double pews at the pulpit shall be appropriated to them.

These two pews were beside the fireplaces!

The numbering of the pews was worked out by the Committee, and "after due consideration of their size and relative position" a rent was set. There were 46 pews in the main part of the church, and these ranged in price from £2 to 10 shillings. Ten pews were in the gallery. These were priced at 15 shillings and 10 shillings. A local painter, John Brogan, was paid to apply the numbers at one penny per pew. The number was to be in black on the inside of each pew door. It is believed that, following further extensions to the church in 1901, these pews were replaced and the new pews had no doors.

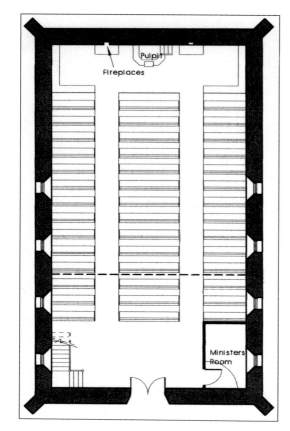

In the nineteenth century many Church pews had doors. Second Omagh was no exception but the old pews were replaced in 1901 with the present pews.

This drawing shows the seating plan in the new Church at 1856. Note that there was a balcony, two fireplaces at the front and no rear entrances. The Ministers room was near the front door as were the stairs to the balcony.

The above drawing shows the probable lay-out of the new church at the time of its rebuild in 1856. The outside walls are the same as those in the main body of the church today. Note that there was a gallery with 10 pews. There was a fireplace on either side of the pulpit and stoves in the porch and in the middle of the church. At this time the choir sang from the gallery. There was no instrumental music and only a limited number of Psalms to choose. The Minister's room was in the porch on the right, and stairs to the gallery were on the left. There were no back doors. The main entrance to the church was where the large blue notice-board is now, situated in the vestibule.

The letting of pews continued to be a regular item of Church Committee business for many years. The practice ceased to be recorded after 1928 with the advent of Free Will Offerings, but most families continued to sit in THEIR pew, and the family names remained on the pews until May 1940, when they were finally removed. With each subsequent refurbishment the name plates, numbers and umbrella stands have gradually been removed. It is now merely habit that guides many families to the same seat each Sunday, but it is noted that a few of the older families still sit in the pews that were let to their ancestors.

Some pews in Trinity c.1920 showing pew name plates, numbers and umbrella stands. These all disappeared during the renovations in 1969.

The area around the Church

The old records of the Church refer regularly to the need to have the walls coloured and the doors and windows painted. In 1897 this work cost £15. These references also relate to works at the Manse after 1860. It is supposed that colouring referred to a type of lime-wash or whitewash that was applied to internal walls as well as to external dashing.

There are also frequent references to the need to have the paths around the church 'gravelled', and it seems to have been the practice for some of the more wealthy members of the Committee to offer from time to time to provide a cart-load of gravel for this purpose.

The Cow Common in 1948.

For most of the nineteenth century the cattle fair was held on the first Saturday of each month on the Fair Green, which stretched from Kevlin Road to the top of Gallows Hill, but often overflowed into the streets, often along John Street as far as the Court-House. Fat cattle were usually sold in Church Street. Later the cattle fair day was changed to the first Tuesday in each month. Some local traders would provide cattle pens or horse stabling in their yards and charge about sixpence to keep the animals for the farmers. The field at the rear of the church was known as the 'Cow Common(s)',and for those who grew up in the area, even through the first half of the twentieth century, Trinity was known as 'the wee church on the Commons'. The more level land above the Cow Common was known as Beacom's Field. As time went by, the areas around the Cow Common and the surrounding district were largely developed for housing purposes. Red-brick houses in the area of Kevlin Road/ New Brighton Terrace were built by private developers in the period 1880-1900, while other public housing covering some of the area of the Cow Common would have been associated with Council building programmes which were enabled after 1920. O'Connor Terrace, named after Councillor O'Connor, father of the solicitor Roddy O'Connor, and Mullan Terrace, named after Councillor Mullan, father of Gerry and Jim Mullan, who had High Street businesses (grocer and pharmacist, respectively), were both built in the late 1920s and early 1930s.

The impact of the new railway

Importantly for this area, the railway from Londonderry, Enniskillen and Dundalk, arrived in Omagh in 1852, 1854 and 1859 respectively followed in 1861 by the Dungannon/Portadown line. This effectively ended the mail coaches to Dublin and elsewhere in Ireland and led to the development or at least redevelopment of John Street and James Street. The Station Hotel* (now the Blind Centre and recently home of the Lagan family) was the first property in James Street. John Street and James Street were named after James and John Galbraith. The Galbraith family came here from Scotland during the Plantation in the early 1600s and acquired land at Clanabogan. Samuel Galbraith was present at the laying of the foundation-stone for the new Second Omagh Church in 1856.

Although built as a hotel, there is some doubt that it ever traded as such. The reason for this is not known.

For many years this horse drinking-trough was located at the bottom of Fairmount Road. This was for the benefit of working horses that had just negotiated the hill from the station. The trough may have replaced a well that was previously located in the grass bank before the O'Connor Terrace houses were built.

New church: opening service - 7 September 1856

The new Church was duly opened by Rev Dr Henry Cooke, DD, LLD from Belfast. There were two services that day, one at noon and another at 7.00 pm. At the morning service there were 413 present and at the evening service 180. It is reported that both congregations were "respectable". The morning collection amounted to £58/18/2 and the evening collection to £19/4/8. Receipts at the door were £7/9/0 and the sale of tickets raised £23/14/0, making the proceeds for the day £109/5/10. Rev Dr Cooke received £3 for his labours. In his address Dr Cooke reminded the congregation of the divine description of Moses: "His eye was not dim, nor was his natural force abated."

After the services several people who had not been able to attend sent subscriptions. These are recorded as follows: James Houston, Murlough, £5; Charles Eccles, Ecclesville, £1; S Gilliland, Derry, £1/1/0; Charles Hunter, Newtownstewart, £1; William McClay, Newtownstewart, £1; and Mrs Monteith, Mullaghmore, 10 shillings.

Financial matters continued to occupy the minds of the committee members for some months as indicated by the following minute.

> **13 October 1856** The builder's final account was for a balance due of £457/13/2 plus extras of £18/13/10. The treasurer announced that when these debts were settled there would be a deficit of £110/12/0. At that point Mr McAdam, the Fund Treasurer, offered to pay the debt in the meantime. This was gratefully accepted by the Committee, and Mr Greer was requested to prepare the necessary Promissory Note.

The practice of accepting formal loans from congregation members seems to have been a regular feature of the church project capital financing in the latter half of the twentieth century. There are several references to actual transactions in the church records.

New sexton's house - 1857

By December 1856 the money to clear this debt had been raised, but it was not settled immediately, in the hope that the Church and Manse Building Fund in Belfast might give an additional grant. The grant does not appear to have been forthcoming, but despite this and remaining debt, the Church Committee resolved to take steps to demolish the Sexton's house and build another house "in the corner of the grounds next to the town". The Committee also agreed to put up suitable railings on the boundary wall and do "such other work as may be necessary." In accordance with recent practices, the congregation was asked once again to provide subscriptions for these new works. It is thought that this Sexton's house was located close to where the kitchen and other extensions are today.

The 1859 Revival

The Revival was a religious 'fever' which swept across the Ulster province and into Southern Ireland in 1859.

In 1857-58 the eastern states of America witnessed this phenomenon, and it was reported that "a revival is now passing over the churches of America such as has not been known since apostolic times". The General Assembly of the Presbyterian Church agreed to send out a circular letter to all Ministers, commending this new movement, and it began in Connor and Ballymena with several prayer meetings each day.

In June 1859 it was reported in the Tyrone Constitution that "services are regularly conducted on the evening of every week-day except Saturday. The attendance is large and an increased number assembles on every successive occasion."

Rev Josias Mitchell of Second Omagh Presbyterian Church was one of the leading clergymen presiding and preaching at many meetings over the next three to four months. Meetings were held at Second Omagh, First Omagh and the Methodist Church.

One meeting in First Omagh, conducted by Rev Mitchell, started at 6.00pm. "The large house was densely crowded; all the aisles were thronged and about 100 persons gathered round the doors and windows." By 9.00 pm Rev Mitchell was bringing the meeting to a close, but suddenly "from various parts of the house sobs were heard which broke into plaintive cries." It was "shortly before eleven o'clock that the congregation was dismissed." Meetings at the Methodist Church were also "densely crowded and the overspill went to the schoolroom underneath the church."

Omagh had its first open-air meeting on Sunday 19 August 1859 at the Railway Market. Fifteen hundred people were assumed to be there, and that evening another meeting was held in First Omagh. On the Wednesday of the same week another open-air meeting was held at noon. It was estimated that about 3,000 people attended and a large number of clergymen. Rev Arnold opened the meeting with singing and prayer, and Rev Mitchell addressed the congregation. He said it was a new thing to see such a meeting held in Omagh, but it was "a happy, a blessed and a glorious thing." After the open-air meeting "many persons retired to the Second Presbyterian Church and the Wesleyan Chapel, for the purpose of further prayer."

On 26 August it was reported that "in the district around the town the movement is progressing with undiminished fervour." Many meetings were conducted in Dromore, Strabane, Newtownstewart, Sixmilecross, Castlederg, Gortin and Beragh. On one occasion in Castlederg an open-air meeting of about 4,000 had to take refuge in the Presbyterian Church and the Methodist Church because of rain, but "after those houses were filled, there were considerably more still outside." This particular meeting was described as follows:

> The scene was such that no mortal pen could describe - it was one long to be remembered. At a late hour Rev Doonan, with great difficulty, could not get the crowded congregation dismissed, even after pronouncing the benediction six times.

A report in the Belfast News Letter at the time sums up the Revival very aptly:

> It is impossible not to notice a great change wrought in whole districts here. There is an

eagerness to attend Divine service, under whatever circumstances, and it is nothing unusual to witness in places where least it might be expected, a congregation gathered into a small apartment for mutual prayer and study of God's Word. Such are the fruits of the revival and 'By their fruits ye shall know them'.

Building Rocklow Manse - 1860

Having undertaken the mammoth task of rebuilding the church in 1856 and a new sexton's house a year later, the Church Committee decided to build a manse, and a new subscription list was proposed in 1858. Instalments were to be paid on 1 December 1858 and 1 December 1859. No details of the design of the house or the actual building are available from the records. There is, however, a list of those people who subscribed - both Church members and local people.

By January 1860, £395 was raised. The builder on this occasion was Mr William Mullan. He received £150 in January 1860 and £250 and other small amounts in February 1860. Even after these payments a debt of £26/14/2 remained and, once again, John McAdam paid the builder the balance out of his own money, in June 1860. Mr McAdam's account with the Church was still in the records in 1866!

This is the first page from a subscription list from 1858-1859. It is typical of similar lists that were kept when the Church needed to raise money for capital building or renovation programmes.

This is one of the earliest photographs of Rocklow Manse believed to be taken around 1920. Note the absence of any development on the right side of the house where the present manse stands.

It is amazing how the members of Second Omagh raised so much money over the 12 years during which much of the building and rebuilding took place. It is obvious from the accounts of that time that not all debt was cleared before they undertook another building project. This was the case again when they decided to rebuild the outhouses at the manse in 1863. (see p.102)

Opening of John Street Hall - 1894

The Church Hall in John Street was opened on 3 April 1894 with a Grand Concert. In its report the Tyrone Constitution said that the hall

> is handsome and commodious and in every way suited for the purpose intended. The interior consists of the ground floor with platform, a gallery over the entrance, and a retiring room beyond the platform, which is fitted up with the necessary conveniences required for soiree purposes. The gallery projects about one-third of the floor area and is capable of accommodating about 100. The front of the gallery is very handsomely finished in pine pannellings with a row of moulded cantilevers closely set together. A lightly recessed Gothic arch gives a finished appearance to the platform end of the building.

> The ventilating system introduced is remarkably perfect - a fact which was noticed and favourably commented upon. In a great many buildings it is nothing short of torture, and beyond this, positively dangerous, to sit in the hot vitiated atmosphere for a couple of hours. This however is not the case in this pretty little hall. During the evening the atmosphere, notwithstanding that the building was crowded to its utmost capacity, was cool and pure throughout - as pure as that outside.

The concert itself was a huge success. With 22 items on the programme, the only adverse comment reported in the Tyrone Constitution related to

> some indiscriminate encoring - senseless in its application and very often the reverse of appreciative expression.

The 'Con' also reported that

> The platform was decorated with a magnificent display of foliage and flowering from the conservatories of Lisnamallard and Clonavon, kindly sent in for the occasion by Mrs Scott and Mrs Dickie. Towards the end the old Jacobite song 'Will ye no come back again', magnificently rendered by Mrs Steele (Strabane), Miss Fleming, Mr Philson and Mr C Mullin, was perhaps the item of the evening.

GRAND CONCERT

IN THE

SECOND OMAGH LECTURE HALL,

JOHN STREET,

WILL BE GIVEN ON

TUESDAY EVENING, 3RD APRIL.

Commencing at Eight o'clock, p.m.

DOORS OPEN AT 7-30.

The Programme will include Songs, Pianoforte or Violin Solos, from the following Ladies and Gentlemen :—

Mrs Steele, Strabane
Miss Grose, Strabane
Miss M'Phail, Glasgow
Mrs Irvine
Miss Fleming
Miss Mullin
Miss Leslie, Cookstown
Mrs Agnew, Belfast
Lt.-Col. Irvine
Mr Charles Mullin
Mr Philson
Rev J M Hamill, M.A.,
and probably
Rev P J Egan, Derry.

PROGRAMME—

PART I.

1 Quartette, Mrs Irvine, Miss Fleming, Mr Mullin, and Mr Philson.
2 Solo, "The Singer and the Song"; Miss Leslie.
3 "Margarita," (L'Ohr), Rev D Morton, B.A., Newtownstewart.
4 Pianoforte Solo, Miss Mullin.
5 Solo, "the Valley by the Sea," (S Adams), Mrs Steele.
6 Violin Solo — Rev J M Hamill, M.A., Londonderry.
7 "The Lights o' London," (Dihl), Miss Grose.
8 "When the Lamp is shattered," (Dolores), Rev Herbert Kelly, B A., Rector of Ballyeglish.
9 "A Summer Night" (Goring Thomas), Mrs Agnew.
10 Solo, — Miss Fleming.
11 Duet, "In the Dusk o' the Twilight," (Parker), Mrs Steele and Miss M Phail.
Interval of five minutes.

PART II.

1 Quartette, — Mrs Irvine, Miss Fleming, Mr Charles Mullin, and Mr Philson.
2 "Marguerite," (Pinsuti), Rev J M Hamill, M.A.
3 Solo, "My Great Grandmother," (Molloy), Mrs Irvine.
4 Solo, "Shipwrecked," (Adams), Rev D Morton, B.A.
5 Solo, — Miss M'Phail.
6 Solo, "The Seventh Royal Fusiliers," (Le Brun) Rev Herbert Kelly.
7 Solo, "Good Bye," (Tosti), Miss Grose.
8 Violin Solo, "Les Cloches de Cornevielle," Rev J M Hamill, M.A.
9 Solo, "Rory Darling," (Hope Temple), Miss Leslie.
10 Solo, "Promise of Life," (Cowan), Mrs Steele.
11 Solo and Chorus, "Will ye no come back again," Mrs Steele, Miss Fleming, Mr Granger, Mr C Mullin.

GOD SAVE THE QUEEN.

Plan of Hall can be seen, and tickets obtained at Messrs Crawford & Co's, and CONSTITUTION Office

As it is expected this Concert will be a great Musical treat the Omagh public are advised not to miss it. 23-3

This programme for the opening of the new hall is typical of similar functions that were a regular feature of Church life until the mid twentieth century.

In the ensuing years this hall was to be used extensively by the Church organisations . A wide range of other activities have also been facilitated by the hall. These include dances, concerts, whist drives, dancing classes, drama, music lessons, auctions and jumble sales. The Boys' Brigade Pipe Band practised there and learned to play under the guidance of Johnny McPoland. The hall was used for drama rehearsals, and in the early 1930s those attending included well- known local people such as Gerry McCausland, Bob Pigott and Walter and Joe Steele. During World War II the hall was taken over by the Army and used for various administrative purposes. Later William Porter held regular furniture auctions in aid of Church funds.

Church extension - 1901

In April 1900 the Committee first viewed plans for the improvement of the heating and the provision of a ceiling in the church. At the same time plans were tabled for extensions and alterations . After much debate it was proposed by Mr T C Dickie that "the extended plans (for all improvements and alterations) be adopted, the cost not to exceed the sum of £800 - a statement to be drawn up to show the members of the congregation what had been decided and that the additional seats would give accommodation to over 100."

These plans provided for a ceiling, two new transepts, a front porch, a Minister's room and two rear entrance doors. The work also included the replacement of the pews and the removal of a gallery which was known to have been present when the new church was built in 1856. It would appear that the Church had been planning an extension for some time, as the financial report on 9 April 1900 showed that "a sum of £622/6/4 had been raised for the various schemes."

On 7 May Mr Foreman, an architect from Londonderry, submitted plans for the alteration and extensions. These were agreed, and he was instructed "to have specifications ready at an early date and to issue advertisements for tenders in the papers."

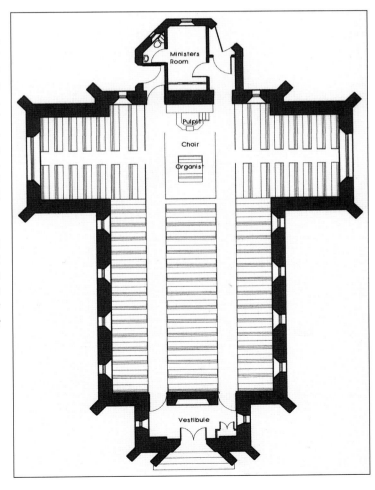

This plan shows the revised pew lay-out following the Church extension in 1901. The balcony has been removed but the pews now go right back to the main Church wall and the new transepts each have 14 pews. The design allowed for 100 extra places. Note: the organ was installed/located as shown after 1903.

It was on 11 June 1900 that, tenders having been received, Mr Hugh Kirk, the Congregational Treasurer, proposed that the price of £850 submitted by Mr William Allison, Killybrack, Omagh be accepted by the Committee. A further scheme for the "hot air" heating of the Church at a cost of £61 was also approved. The contract prepared by the architect was signed by the builder and by every member of the Church Committee, with a completion date of 1 February 1901 being agreed. The Committee members in 1900 were: Messrs Robert Lyons(Omagh), William Dale, James Lyons, John Fallows, Hugh Kirk, James Campbell, Robert W McAdam, John Barr, William J McClelland, J K McConnell, William Houston, John J Kerr, William McFarlane, John White and Joseph Wilson. Elders at that time were: Joseph Anderson, T C Dickie, R D Swan and T J McAdam.

In October 1900 the Committee agreed with the architect's specification for the design and positioning of a gas lighting scheme for the church. The scheme included "gas pendants with shades and incandescent burners at 50 shillings each." It is probable that, prior to that time, the church, for evening worship in winter, was lit by candles and oil lamps.

During the building, the need for extra windows was identified. New windows would be required at either side of the pulpit and in the new front and rear porches. It is recorded that, within days, an anonymous donor had agreed to pay for their installation. The final cost of the alterations and extensions was £1,376/18/9. Of that sum £970/7/0 had been raised before the official reopening on 25 October 1901. During the period of the work and afterwards the Committee benefited from low-interest loans from one of its members, Mr William Dale. Such a loan is recorded in August 1901, when the sum was £200 at 3.5 %. Another loan of £100 is recorded in March 1902.

The contract with Mr Allison seems to have ended somewhat acrimoniously when the builder was offered, by the Church Committee, "an additional sum of about £106 as a gratuity for the substantial way the work was carried out." The Church minutes record that "this proposal was not very generously received by the contractor, who evidently thought the present too small and neither accepted nor declined it but asked the meeting to think over the matter." The minute also explains that Mr Allison had already received a cheque from Rev George Thompson, the Minister, for £50 in addition to the contract price of £850 and extras totalling £204. Any differences seem to have been mended through time because Mr Allison was elected to the Church Committee in 1906!

Before the official opening on 25 October 1901 linoleum was laid along the aisles of the church. All members who desired to retain their old pew were so permitted, and the first four pews in the new right transept were reserved for the military personnel attending Church.

From 'Second Omagh' to 'Trinity'

It was in October 1908 that Rev Morrow proposed that consideration should be given to changing the name of the Church from Second Omagh "to that of a more suitable and appropriate name". Although the seed had been sown, any contemplated change was postponed. It was to be September 1910 when the Church Committee returned to this topic and agreed that the name should be changed to Trinity Presbyterian Church, Omagh. Interestingly, the first two actions taken by the Committee of "Trinity" Church were, firstly, to arrange to have the name on the Church notice-board changed and, secondly, to have a bank account opened in the name of 'Trinity Presbyterian Church' and to arrange for the transfer of Church accounts.

Electric lighting in church

A suggestion to replace the gas lights with an electric scheme was first mooted in 1931. It was proposed that estimates should be obtained, but several members of the Committee suggested an amendment that this matter should be delayed for a year or two, the Church continuing with gas lighting. The amendment was defeated, and it was left to Mr R D Swan and Mr T J McAdam to move "that we have church buildings lighted with electric light." Mr Swan was appointed as convener of a sub-committee to gather specifications and tenders. On 24 August 1931 he presented to the Committee a comprehensive report, which was unanimously adopted. The lighting contract was won by Messrs May of Great James Street, Londonderry. Sadly, Mr Swan died in January 1932 and it is unlikely that he ever saw the church lights switched on.

Church heating

The heating of the first church would have been by coal or turf fire and little else. We know that in 1856 two fireplaces were provided in the new church, on either side of the pulpit. Two additional heating stoves were provided - one in the porch and one centrally under the gallery. There was no rear entrance until 1901, when the fireplaces were replaced by back doors and the first "church central heating" was introduced. The heat came from a new boiler in the church basement and was referred to, at that time, as a "hot air system". It provided a flow of hot air from the boiler through grills in the church aisle floors. Many who have seen old photographs of the church will have noticed that it had on the roof not only a bell tower but also, towards the back, something that looked like a spire. The spire-like structure was, in fact, a ventilator, incorporated into the building when the central heating was installed in 1901. In January 1927 there was a great storm which caused a lot of damage to the roof of the church. In considering this, Mr R D Swan, Congregational Treasurer, and Mr T J McAdam, Clerk of Session, proposed that the ventilator on the roof be removed in conjunction with the extensive repairs that were needed. Any pictures or photographs in which the ventilation spire appears can therefore be dated within the period 1901-1927.

This photograph taken around 1910 shows clearly one of the heating grills in the aisle of the Church. Hot air came up into the Church through such grills. Note also the absence of organ pipes.

From 1901 to 1927 Trinity Church had a distinctive ventilation tower on its roof. These two photographs illustrate the "before and after" appearance of the building.

The "hot air system" was duly replaced by a hot water system, with pipes laid along the walls and aisles. Even this system was very demanding as it required frequent boiler maintenance and considerable manual work. The work entailed lighting the boiler with kindling and coke no later than four o'clock on Sunday mornings. During the winter of 1912 the Sexton was instructed to light the boiler at 10 o'clock every Saturday night.

It was in 1933, following the success of the electric lighting, that it was first proposed that Trinity should explore the possibility of having electric heating in the church. A sub-committee, appointed to check on this, reported favourably and recommended that "we install electric heating to a specification supplied by the Northern Ireland Electricity Board". Subsequently a tender received from John Dowling for £203 was accepted.

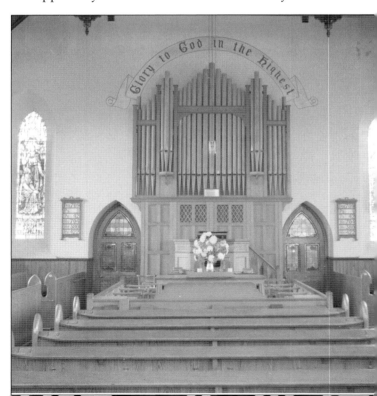

Later, in the 1960s, the heating system was once more changed to one based on electrically heated tubes in each pew. This system remains today, and the present congregation can only speculate on the frequently cold circumstances that our forefathers experienced when sermons were much longer.

Trinity Church interior c 1955.
The scripture verse was on the front wall from 1930. It was not replaced following the major renovations in 1969.

Scripture on wall behind pulpit

In July 1930 the Church property was undergoing a comprehensive re-paint. At the time of setting the contract Mr Joseph Wilson proposed and Mr T J McAdam seconded that a verse of Scripture be inscribed on the front wall above the organ pipes. Some of the present congregation will remember this as a feature in Trinity. However, it transpired that the back wall was subject to sweating, condensation and consequent flaking of paint. It was difficult to maintain the writing in those circumstances, so in 1969, when the church was once more subjected to major renovation, the verse of Scripture was not replaced and the wall was painted in a 'Presbyterian' blue.

Other electrics

The 1930s were the age of introducing electricity to Trinity. Following the installation of electric lighting and heating in the church, electric light was also installed in the manse.

In 1936 Mr Harold McCauley proposed that an electric light be installed over the pulpit as the light on the reading desk was inadequate. This was the origin of the light fitting that still hangs above the pulpit.

The Dunlopillo cushions

In June 1952, in conjunction with the Church's bicentenary, the Committee decided to have the seats covered "with some suitable cushioning". A circular letter was sent to every family, and collectors were appointed for the various districts. The letter provoked much discussion among the congregation, with not everyone being in favour of the proposed scheme. The mood of some is reflected by the following poem attributed to Mrs H M Price, a well- known local poet and a Church member:

Dunlopillo Pews

We're getting luxury minded
In Trinity Church affairs
With cushions and with carpets
On which to say our prayers.
The man up in the pulpit
Will find it hard to keep
These Dunlopillo sitters
From falling fast asleep.

"The heathen in their darkness"
How sad their lot must be
No light, no help, no gospel
Except through you and me.
No Dunlopillo cushions
For this most needy race,
No messenger to bring them
The Story of God's Grace.

Can we who know the story
So old yet ever new,
Sit back enjoying comfort
And blessings not a few,
Oh no! the cause of missions
They can no more refuse
Who sit at ease and worship
In Dunlopillo pews.

HM Price

Church hall extension - 1956

After discussions lasting about one year it was finally agreed, in June 1956, to proceed with the provision of an extension to the Church hall. This was enabled by the purchase of some additional land from the Council in March 1955. The plans for the extension were prepared by a Church Committee member, Mr Edgar Weir, and the sub-committee with responsibility for the project was: Messrs Weir, J C White, Arthur McFarland, R Parke and H McCauley. The total estimate for the work was £2,507/4/0. Prominent in the building works were Ronnie Orr (now an Elder) and James Monteith and Charles McFarland, fathers of present Church Committee members Raymond Monteith and Artie McFarland (also an Elder).

At the outset Rev Pinkerton asked the congregation if anyone would volunteer to help with the building works. Over 70 men and 20 women volunteered to assist. Such was the enthusiasm and camaraderie that a Christmas dinner was held in the Church hall before the building works were completed.

Christmas dinner in the new hall extension 1956. Note the rough, unfinished concrete walls. Included are Mrs Millar, Arthur McFarland, RA Parke, Wm Martin and Mrs Martin.

A view through the ceiling rafters of the new hall kitchen. The Church entrance can be seen outside in the background.

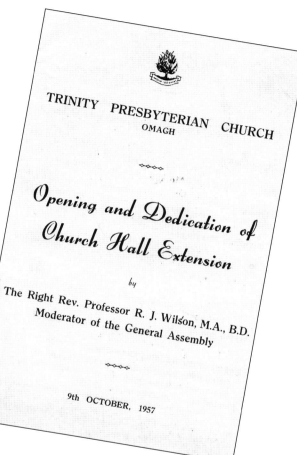

TRINITY PRESBYTERIAN CHURCH

OMAGH

Opening and Dedication of Church Hall Extension

by

The Right Rev. Professor R. J. Wilson, M.A., B.D.
Moderator of the General Assembly

9th OCTOBER, 1957

New Church car park - 1965

In October 1961 the Committee became aware of a Council proposal to construct a new road at the back of the church. This triggered an enquiry by the Church to the Council about the possibility of acquiring a portion of the Fair Green for a car park. After much correspondence with the Council over the next few years, the District Valuer eventually placed a valuation of £200 on the land, which was duly purchased by resolution of the Committee on 21 March 1965. This land forms the existing car park. For the first 15 years it was gravelled. In 1980 the gravel was replaced with a tarmacadam surface.

The Church car park area was acquired in 1965. From 1965 to 1980 the car park surface was gravel. This was improved with tar-macadam around 1980.

Internal renovations - 1969

Throughout its life, the church building had been plagued with penetrating dampness, causing the interior decor to deteriorate frequently and necessitating constant redecoration. In 1969 it was decided to undertake extensive renovation of the interior of the church. This involved the total re-plastering of the walls, including the insertion of a vertical damp-proof course. Until that time a record of the Church's history had been carved into the window-sills. Sadly, these sills were accidentally destroyed at that time, but their information, having been previously noted by Rev Pinkerton, was transferred to a new information board in the alcove at the vestibule. During these renovations the church was closed for Sunday worship during September, October and November. Services were held in First Omagh Church, commencing at 10.00 am. It was also at that time that the umbrella stands, fittings and pew numbers were finally removed.

Painting the pews 'white'

It was following the above renovations that the pews were painted light grey. This fairly radical and controversial decision was taken on the recommendation of the eminent architect Mr McCormack from Londonderry, who also recommended that the front wall should be painted blue. This prompted quite a debate among the congregation, with many advocating a return to traditional wood-grain colours. However, as the colour scheme had been recommended by Mr McCormack, it remained and, to this day, continues to be a much-remarked-upon feature of the church. A proposal to have a wood-carved 'burning bush' on the wall above the organ pipes did not go ahead. At this time also the aisle covering was replaced at a cost of £15/6/3.

Trinity's light grey pews remain a popular talking point among members and visitors.

It is clear that, as in the nineteenth century so also in the twentieth century, the Church was blessed with strong decision makers and businessmen amongst its members. These people were contributing practically to the development of business and commerce in the Omagh area as well as assisting the Church by giving the benefit of their collective experiences. In the twentieth century these included business names such as McConnell, Dickie, Black, Cathcart, Dick, Todd, Lyons, Monteith, McCauley, McFarland, Porter, White, Swan, Armstrong and Coote while being increasingly supported by leaders in the public sector such as R Parke, AH Coote, D. MacKenzie, J. Wallace and many others.

The Church bell

The Church building had a bell tower for 118 years - but no bell. In 1974 a bell was installed and dedicated in an event unique in the Church's history in that it had been presented by the Church of Ireland. The bell weighs about one hundredweight and was about 150 years old when it arrived in Omagh. It formerly hung in Stranooden Parish Church, County Monaghan and was formally handed over to Trinity by the then Bishop of Clogher, Rt Rev R W Heavener.*

The bell was erected by ex-Service men and women of the congregation and was dedicated by Bishop Heavener and the Moderator of Omagh Presbytery, Rev J Davison, Drumquin on 24 April 1974. The service was conducted by the Minister, Rev R W W Clarke, whose initiative had secured the gift. The large congregation of about 400 included representatives of the civic and community life of the town. Also present were two former Ministers of Trinity, Very Rev Dr J H Gibson and Rev R H Pinkerton, from whom there were expressions of goodwill.

In his address, Bishop Heavener said that the bell was a memorial to those who had died in the two world wars and to the people who had suffered and died in the troubles of that time in Northern Ireland. He hoped that it would not only call the faithful to prayer but also soon be used to ring out the period of trouble and violence and ring in an age of peace and goodwill between all people and that it might be a milestone on the road to closer union and greater fellowship between their two Churches.

The bell was installed structurally by Mr Maurice Taylor and electrically by Mr Ronald McCrea (Pettigo). At the service, standard-bearers from the various ex-Service associations were present, as well as those representing the 1st Omagh Boys' Brigade and Girls' Brigade.

*(Bishop Heavener is a brother-in-law of the late Mrs E Coote, who was a member of Trinity congregation, and an uncle of two present members, Jean Coote and Margaret Simms.)

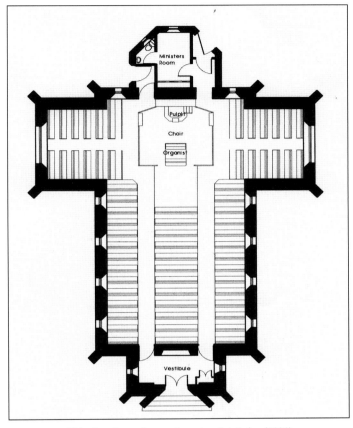

This plan shows the pew layout as it is today (2004).
Note the widening of the choir enclosure, the removal of one pew from each transept and two pews at the front middle.

The people of Second Omagh/Trinity

Early Second Omagh families

ALTHOUGH Trinity Presbyterian Church (formerly Second Omagh) has been in existence since 1754, we cannot find any records before the Baptism Records, which started in 1821. In 1751, approximately 50 families left the Omagh congregation and asked the Synod of Ulster to be "erected into a separate congregation". The men reported as leading this separation were Mr William Scott and a Mr James Nixon. However, in the indenture to purchase the land for a new Church the names of John Scott of Strathroy, Thomas Rodger of Edergole and William McConnell of Tattyneur are on the document that is signed by J Maxwell and John Nixon.

The keeping of records was not compulsory for Presbyterian Ministers until 1819, and it was not until 1845 that the recording of Protestant marriages became law under the Civil Registration Scheme. Civil registration of births, deaths and Catholic marriages became compulsory from 1 January 1864.

As Presbyterian Ministers came under the Penal Laws by 1704 it was illegal for them to perform marriages of members of their congregations until 1782. By 1845 they were allowed to marry a Presbyterian and a member of the Church of Ireland. Any marriages prior to those dates may well be documented in the records of the nearest Church of Ireland establishment.

The Baptism records for Trinity are contained in two books. The first spans the years 1821-1942; the second is from 1943 to the present. Naturally the first book is the more interesting, particularly the earlier years. It is written mostly in black ink. Some Ministers wrote clearly and carefully, using a ruler to draw out the columns; others drew columns freehand or not at all. The Rev Josias Mitchell (at Second Omagh 1842-1879) recorded the first 10 years of his Baptisms at the back of the book and then reverted to the proper order at the front. It was also during Rev Mitchell's time that a few entries from the years 1852 and 1854 were cut out.

When given the opportunity to peruse old records it is always worthwhile to search every page, even when you think you have reached the logical end. This is how we discovered that the 'missing 10 years' were located at the back of the book.

Other interesting entries were a family of six children by the name of Montgomery, whose names were all entered on the Baptism Register on the day of the youngest child's baptism, which was 26 July 1902. Rev Thompson noted "Entered at parents' request. All these children (5) were baptised at Episcopal Church." We believe that John Montgomery and his family moved from Londonderry at that time. John was later to become the Church sexton.

During a short vacancy in the Church - January 1898 to March 1898 - Rev Samuel Paul, Minister of Gillygooley, conducted three baptisms. From April 1918 to November 1918 a Rev McFarland carried out baptisms. This was during the time of the ministry of Rev H W

Morrow. Details from these early records of baptisms, communicants and marriages are included in **Appendix 3**.

On a lighter note Rev Thomas McAfee Hamill made an unusual entry on 9 February 1881:

> I solemnly promise in dependence on Divine strength to abstain from
> the use of all intoxicating drinks as beverages.
> Signed: (made his mark with an 'X') Henry Kearney
> Dated at Coneywarren, Omagh, 9 February 1881.

Rev Hamill may also have been the person who wrote a full page and a half of "Extracts from P O Guide, October 1883". This gave a detailed description of how letters were transported around the world.

Church records are a very valuable source of family connections, particularly before Civil Registration (1845 for Protestant marriages and 1864 for births and all marriages). They become even more important when we remember that the Census Records, which commenced in Ireland in 1821, were all lost, one way or another, so that the 1901 census is the first complete one to exist.

Present Trinity families

As Omagh is the county town of Tyrone, its population over the last century has been transient, with many public-sector workers being subject to regular transfer. The same applied to many other posts, particularly in security and banking. The congregation of Second Omagh and Trinity has reflected this trend and seen steady change, with the departure of some families balanced by the arrival of others. In more recent years the drift from the country towards the towns saw an increase in the congregation that is now being counterbalanced by the spread of 'suburbia' right out to adjacent villages. In a recent survey we found that the average 'life' of a typical family in the present congregation is 38.78 years.

The surnames of present families are: Adair, Adams, Alexander, Allen, Anderson, Armstrong, Atchison, Baillie, Barbour, Barron, Bell, Black, Bloomfield, Booth, Bradley, Breslin, Browne, Buchanan, Burke, Caldwell, Campbell, Campton, Candon, Carey, Carson, Cathcart, Chesney, Chisholm, Clarke, Clements, Clyde, Colbourne, Colhoun, Cooke, Coote, Coulson, Crawford, Cummins, Cuthbertson, Davis, Dodds, Donald, Donnell, Dorrian, Duff, Duffield, Duncan, Dunn, Eccles, Elkin, Elliott, Espie, Ewing, Faithful, Fallows, Fenwick, Ferguson, Finlay, Folliard, Fulton, Fyffe, Gallagher, Gaston, Gilchrist, Gilfillan, Gillespie, Gilmore, Gilmour, Ginn, Gordon, Graham, Gregg, Halkyard, Hall, Hamilton, Hannigan, Heaney, Hemphill, Henderson, Henry, Herron, Hetherington, Hill, Hughes, Hussey, Irwin, Jardine, Johnston, Kane, Kerr, Keys, Kincaid, Kinloch, Knox, Large, Leitch, Little, Magee, Maginnis, Maguire, Malcolmson, Marshall, Maxwell, McCandless, McCauley, McCay, McClelland, McClung, McCombe, McConnell, McCrudden, McCurdy, McCutcheon, McDonald, McElhinney, McFarland, McGeagh, McGrew, McGurk, McElwaine, McIvor, McKean, McKelvey, McKernaghan, McKibbin, McKnight, McNickle, Millar, Milligan, Monteith, Montgomery, Moore, Morrison, Neary, Nelson, O'Donnell, Oliver, Orr, Parke, Patterson, Perkins, Pollock,

Porter, Quinn, Reid, Robertson, Ross, Sayers, Scanlon, Scobie, Scott, Shannon, Simms, Smith, Smyth, Somerville, Stewart, Strong, Stubbs, Thompson, Ward, Watson, Wilson, Woodside, Young,

An indication of the diversity of backgrounds of the current congregation members is seen by examining a list of former places of worship. Our members include people who came to us from the following 54 Churches:

Ardstraw Presbyterian Church
Artigarvan Presbyterian Church
Aughentaine Presbyterian Church
Badoney Presbyterian Church
Ballykelly Presbyterian Church
Ballynahatty Presbyterian Church
Bolton United Reform Church
Castlederg Church of Ireland
Cavanaleck Presbyterian Church, Fivemiletown
Cappagh Parish Church
Clogher Presbyterian Church
Clogherney Presbyterian Church
Comber Church of Ireland, County Down
Corrick Presbyterian Church
Creevan Presbyterian Church
Douglas Bridge Presbyterian Church
Dromore Presbyterian Church
Drumnakilly Church of Ireland
Drumquin Presbyterian Church
Drumragh Parish Church
Dungannon Presbyterian Church
Faughanvale Presbyterian Church
Fergus Church of Scotland, Ayrshire, Scotland
Fintona Presbyterian Church
Fireduff Presbyterian Church, Crossmaglen
First Castlederg Presbyterian Church
First Comber Presbyterian Church, County Down
First Omagh Presbyterian Church
Fivemiletown Parish Church
Gillygooley Presbyterian Church
Gilnahirk Presbyterian Church, Belfast
Glenelly Presbyterian Church
Glenhoy Presbyterian Church
Gortin Presbyterian Church
Gransha Presbyterian Church, Comber, County Down
Great James Street Presbyterian Church, Londonderry
Greenan Church of Ireland, Gortin

Holy Trinity Church, Dromore
Langfield Parish Church, Drumquin
Mall Presbyterian Church, Armagh
Mountjoy Presbyterian Church
Newtowncunningham Presbyterian Church, County Donegal
Newtownstewart Presbyterian Church
Second Castlederg Presbyterian Church
Second Kilkeel Presbyterian Church, County Down
Sixmilecross Church of Ireland
Sixmilecross Presbyterian Church
Seskinore Presbyterian Church
Strand Presbyterian Church, Londonderry
St Columba's Parish Church, Omagh
St Salvator's Church of Ireland, Glaslough, County Monaghan
Trinity Presbyterian Church, Letterkenny
Ulsterville Presbyterian Church, Belfast
Waterside Presbyterian Church, Londonderry

The Church has also assembled the following biographical notes on some of the people who, through the years, have served it well in various capacities. They are listed in birth date order.

James Greer Senior (1775-1872)

James Greer was the Senior Elder in Second Omagh congregation at the time of his death. He was possibly also a Clerk of Session for a considerable time. It was a 'James Greer Junior' who laid the foundation-stone for the rebuilt church in 1856. James Sen lived to the age of 97 years. He was a solicitor by profession and a very wealthy man. He was the local and a lifetime director of the first bank in Omagh, the Provincial, from its establishment in 1829. He was distinguished not only for his wealth but also for his liberality, in which his example was followed by his family. James's obituary reflects this when it states that his was

> a most useful life in active, honourable industry, during which time he maintained, with rich and poor alike, the most unblemished character for sterling integrity and honest worth. So long as his strength permitted, he supported every local improvement and charity connected with Omagh and district. ... Although of strong convictions, he never unnecessarily intruded them on others; whilst he freely accorded to those who differed from him the same liberty of thought and right of private judgement which he asserted for himself. He was imbued with the deepest religious feeling, and gladly extended the right hand of fellowship to all evangelical Christians, following as his highest example and guide the late venerable Dr Cooke, of whose friendship he was ever proud.

From this it is clear that James Greer was the influence behind Dr Cooke's visit to Omagh to officially open the new church in 1856.

Joseph McKnight (1790-1866)

Joseph McKnight came to Omagh from Augher about 1810 and set up as a woollen draper. He was later appointed the first Clerk to Omagh Poor Law Union. One of his daughters, Susan, married Rev Robert Wallace, then in Scotstown (1853) but later in Coleraine and, most significantly, Minister in Second Omagh from 1890 to1898. Joseph's son, William Johnston McKnight, succeeded him as Clerk of the Guardians and held that position for about 30 years. Joseph is buried at Clogher.

Robert Ferguson (1808-1891)

Robert Ferguson was an Elder in the Presbyterian Church for 60 years, the last 40 in Second Omagh. He was born in Corrick, near Plumbridge, and established a business in Dungannon before joining the County Treasurer's office in 1831 as an accountant, a post that he filled until he was 81 years old. In 1851 he moved to Campsie Road, Omagh, where he stayed until his death.

William Johnston McKnight (1825-1898)

William McKnight was Clerk to Omagh Poor Law Union for about 30 years. This position was the equivalent of Chief Executive of the District or County Council in modern terms. The McKnight family were influential in the decision to demolish the old church and build a new church on the same site in 1856. In fact, William McKnight's brother-in-law, Alexander Hardy, was the architect for the project. William's daughter Elizabeth married T J McAdam, of whom more will be told later in this publication.

John J White (1835 -1906)

John J White was an Elder in Second Omagh Church for a great many years. He was a prosperous farmer and lived at Beagh, Omagh. It is reported that he was "a favourite in the district where he lived, being esteemed by all classes of the community for his uprightness and straightforward manner on all occasions." He was a Town Commissioner for some years, including 1882.

Thomas Coulter Dickie (1838-1908)

T C Dickie was an Elder of the Church and a trustee of the Commutation Fund of the General Assembly of the Presbyterian Church in Ireland. He was first elected to the Church Committee in 1868. He was also Superintendent of the Sunday School for 30 years, and there is a wall plaque in the church paying tribute to his life and work therein. Largely through his efforts, the Boy's Brigade in Omagh was revived in 1906, and he was its President until his death. T C Dickie was also a trustee of Omagh Young Men's Christian

Association (YMCA) and a member of the Board of Governors of Omagh Academy. He was a native of Dundalk. He came to Omagh in 1862 and established a legal practice. In 1892 he entered into partnership with Mr R H Carson, and the firm practised as 'Dickie and Carson'. Thomas Dickie lived at Clonavon, Hospital Road, Omagh.

William Dale (1840-1913)

William Dale was a prominent member of the congregation for many years. In 1898 he agreed to take over as Congregational Secretary from T J McAdam "for a few months". He was finally relieved of the post by John Knox McConnell in 1903. William traded as a grocer and baker at John Street, Omagh, premises later to be occupied by others including Mr Fred Todd. He lived at John Street and Crevenagh and was reported to be one of the most prosperous and progressive businessmen of his day. This is supported by Church records that reveal frequent low-interest loans by him to the Church during the time of Church hall development and Church extension, namely 1894-1902. In his obituary he is described as "of a quiet, retiring nature, friendly disposed to everyone, most courteous and upright in his dealings and a much-liked personality." William was one of the last Town Commissioners in Omagh before the formation of Urban and Rural District Councils. His son, Roberts Dale, also served on the Church Session and Committee.

Joseph Anderson (1841-1921)

Joseph Anderson was the founder in 1865 of one of Omagh's best-known and most successful businesses, later to be known as J B Anderson and Co Ltd. For many years he was the Senior Elder in the congregation, but his work for the Presbyterian Church extended as far as the General Assembly, where he was highly regarded. He represented Omagh Presbytery with distinction and was one of several local laymen who pioneered a then revolutionary scheme to secure better incomes for Ministers, who were then experiencing difficulty in maintaining their dependants in reasonable comfort and respect in the community.

He was one of the key people who made the visionary decisions in the 1890s and the early twentieth century to build a new Sexton's house and a new Church hall and to carry out a major extension of the church itself. Joseph Anderson paid for a pew in the church for himself and his family and also one for his staff. He served in Second Omagh/Trinity under the leadership and guidance of seven Ministers.

A most active man, he gave his time willingly to many public causes. He was a Town Commissioner in the period before 1898 and was one of the first members of the new Urban Council, serving for more than 20 years. He was one of the pioneers of the movement for technical education in Omagh and sat on the first such committee for 20 years. On top of all that, he was Captain of a flourishing Boys' Brigade Company, a founding member of Omagh YMCA and one of the founding members of Omagh Golf Club, where he was a former captain. Joseph Anderson's son, Captain J B Anderson, succeeded him as Managing Director of the business and also as a member of Committee in Trinity Church. Captain Anderson served in the 1914-18 war, where he was wounded and consequently died at a comparatively early age in 1928.

Hugh Kirk (1841-1914)

Hugh Kirk was a member of the Committee of Trinity Presbyterian Church for many years. It is reported that he was always anxious to further the Church's welfare and to feel that it was prospering. He was Congregational Treasurer from before 1889 until his death in 1914. During his term of office some of the most important improvements were carried out to the Church buildings. The church was enlarged and a new hall and meeting rooms were erected.

Mr Hugh Kirk came to Omagh from Newtownards about 1860. Between the ages of 20 and 30 he established a prosperous Boot and Shoe Warehouse at 38A High Street and became one of the leading merchants in the town. He lived at 3 Sedan Avenue before building a new house at Ashdene, Campsie Road. At some time after 1871 he went into partnership with his brother-in-law, Robert Douglas Swan, and the business name changed to Kirk and Swan. When he died in 1914 his business was acknowledged as the longest-established in Omagh, reflecting the great changes that had taken place over that period.

He was known in the town as a man of the highest integrity and uprightness and was held in high esteem by many. He took a prominent part in public affairs. He was a Town Commissioner and, following the creation of Omagh as an urban district, he was elected as one of the first Council members. Although he represented Unionism on the Council, it is reported that he "was not, however, of intolerant disposition, and was greatly respected by his political opponents of the time, with whom he ever desired to live in peace on terms of equality." Sadly his tombstone lies broken at Dublin Road cemetery.

Armer J Ferguson (c 1848-1929)

Armer Ferguson was a member of the Church Committee from 1885 to 1927 and Congregational Secretary from before 1885 until 1893. At the time of his death he was described as one of the oldest and most experienced public officials in the county. He was in charge of the Rates Department and was a former employee of the Town Commissioners, as well as of Tyrone County Council, which superseded that body. He was also an accomplished farmer. He lived at Fortlands, Coneywarren, Omagh.

John Barr (c 1852-1904)

John Barr was a member of Trinity Church Committee when the Church building was enlarged by the addition of a vestibule and transepts. It is reported that he was the first person to offer financial support for the project, an action that "stimulated the other gentlemen on the committee". It is also reported that "his kindly presence in the councils of the Church was like a ray of sunshine and that his words, deliberate and well reasoned out, invariably carried weight". John Barr was proprietor of the Tyrone Constitution for about nine years, having joined the staff of the paper some 31 years earlier. He lived at Holmview Terrace, Campsie, Omagh. A gifted journalist, he expanded the Tyrone Constitution to eight pages. His obituary in the paper states:

> His policy was trenchant criticism of a wrong, and suggested remedial measures; according praise to those that merited it, even although their opinions were diametrically opposed to his, and above all things, he was just. ... In public affairs he took more than a passing interest, although not identifying himself with any party. The natural consequence was that his leading article was free from that religious or political prejudice characteristic of other organs, and the result was that it was read equally by Protestants and Roman Catholics, and amongst the latter he numbered hosts of friends, all attracted to him by his genial and loving personality.

T J McAdam (1856-1945)

T J McAdam was a central figure in the history of Second Omagh and subsequently Trinity congregation. He was Clerk of Session for 52 years (from 1890 until 1942) and was Congregational Secretary for some years, including the period 1894-1897. These were years of significant development and expansion of Second Omagh, when a new Church hall was built, transepts were added and other improvements made to the church.

T J McAdam is best remembered for his musical talent. A member of Trinity choir for more than 80 years, he was choir leader for more than 50 years, during which time instrumental music was introduced, followed by the installation of a new pipe organ in 1940. He was an outstanding vocalist and occupied his usual seat in the choir until about one week before his death.

One little light-hearted story illustrates, to some degree, the dedication and nature of T J McAdam. Every Sunday he brought two bags of sweets, one for the Minister and one for the Organist and choir. Also, on Armistice Sunday, he provided a poppy for every member of the choir. The practice of providing sweets within the choir continues today.

Mr McAdam lived at Campsie Road, Omagh (present site of the British Legion Club). He was a pharmacist and a senior partner in Messrs McAdam and Bates (chemists), High Street. That firm had been established about 1845 by his father, John McAdam, who was joined by Mr M V Bates about 1910. T J McAdam was also Registrar of Tyrone County Hospital for 60 years and apothecary to the Tyrone and Fermanagh Hospital for more than 40 years.

In 1947, in token of their gratitude, the members of Trinity installed a Communion Table and Chair as a permanent memorial to his work and worth. Interestingly, T J McAdam married Elizabeth Johnston McKnight, daughter of another staunch Second Omagh family. Elizabeth's aunt, Susan McKnight, married Rev Robert Wallace around 1853. Rev Wallace was to be Minister in Second Omagh from 1890 to 1898.

John Knox McConnell (1863-1935)

John Knox McConnell was a member of the Trinity Church Committee from 1894 until 1935. He served as Congregational Secretary from 1903 to 1928. He was one of the key decision-makers when the church was extended in 1901. On his death he was described as "one who enjoyed the friendship and confidence of his brethren in legal circles, and the goodwill of hundreds of the poorer classes in and around Omagh, whom he had frequently befriended." Mr McConnell was one of the best-known and most highly esteemed professional gentlemen in the town. He was a solicitor by profession. He had a well-established legal practice at 41 High Street (above McAdam and Bates, Chemists) and, from 1902, at 1 John Street before being joined, in 1919, by Captain W H Fyffe, when the business name changed to McConnell and Fyffe, retaining its offices at John Street. The firm continues to practise in Omagh, now at 21 Church Street. Mr McConnell was also a founder member of the YMCA in the town and held all offices in that organisation. He was a fine salmon fisherman, highly respected for his skills, and was an accomplished marksman, competing at rifle shooting at the highest levels in Ulster.

John Knox McConnell's mother was formerly Jane Ashfield, daughter of Knox Ashfield, who died in 1887. It is known that Knox Ashfield was a member of the congregation in 1854. John's father, Robert McConnell, was one of the oldest and most respected inhabitants of Omagh when he died in 1904. He was for many years proprietor of the Stewart Arms Hotel before taking to farming in later life. It is from these families that the names Ashfield Terrace and McConnell Place are derived.

J K McConnell himself lived at Ashfield Villa, on the site now occupied by the Homebase development.

Robert Douglas Swan (1865-1932)

Robert Douglas Swan taught in Sunday School at Trinity Presbyterian Church for over 50 years and was its Superintendent for more than 20 years. He was elected to the Church Committee in 1893 and became an Elder, serving as Congregational Treasurer from 1914 until his death in 1932. His work for Second Omagh is commemorated on a brass wall plaque in the left transept.

Mr Swan was born in Buncrana but came to Omagh in his late teens to join his brother-in-law-to-be, Mr Hugh Kirk, in his footwear business, The Boot and Shoe Warehouse. They later traded as Kirk and Swan until the death of Mr Kirk in 1914, after which Mr Swan entered into a new partnership with Mr Robert Mitchell of Campsie Road, Omagh to trade as Swan and Mitchell, 26 High Street.

R D Swan was a local magistrate. His obituary in the Tyrone Constitution states :

> Mr Swan was a gentleman whom to know was to love. He was kind-hearted, generous, sympathetic and benevolent. Endowed with all the graces of a true Christian gentleman, he frequently aided the distressed in their difficulties and in a most in-ostentatious way won the enduring affection of many in lowly positions in life by his innate goodness of heart and acts of charity.

The current Church Secretary, John McCandless, is Douglas Swan's great grand nephew.

Arthur W McFarland (1869-1964)

Arthur McFarland was an Elder in Trinity for about 40 years. He lived at Dublin Road, Omagh. His working life was spent in the drapery and outfitting business, first in Beragh and then in Omagh. His hobby was ornithology. He had a great knowledge of cage-birds and exhibited extensively in the North-West. His nephew, also named Arthur, was Clerk of Session from 1976 to 1980. Arthur's business in High Street is now run by the Russell family, who were close relatives.

Joseph Wilson (c 1870-1954)

Joseph Wilson was a member of the Church Committee for 54 years. He was at one time elected to the Eldership of the Church but declined this honour. He lived at Glenalt, Dublin Road, Omagh. Mr Wilson's son, Victor John Frackleton, was killed in action on 17 October 1918, and there is a brass plaque to his memory in Trinity Church. Joseph Wilson came to Omagh about 1894, following which he joined Mr Frank Crawford as a partner in the well-established hardware and stationery business, which subsequently traded as Crawford and Wilson. On the death of Frank Crawford, Joseph Wilson became its Managing Director. He was a local magistrate and a member of the Grand Jury. In 1953, coronation year, he was High Sheriff. He was also a former President of Omagh Chamber of Commerce.

David Black (1873-1945)

David Black was a member of the Church Committee for 10 years before ill-health forced him to reduce his activities and workload. A native of Randalstown, he worked in Limavady and Dublin before establishing, in 1904, a business in Omagh that later became known throughout Ireland and further afield as Black's of Omagh. He was a hardware and furniture merchant and an auctioneer.

David Black also served as a member of Omagh District Council. He was one of the best-known figures in commercial circles and was a familiar and popular personality in the town. On his death, his son, Desmond, returned to Omagh to run the business. Desmond Black is a current member of Trinity congregation, having served for many years on the Church Committee and as a Ruling Elder.

Robert Andrew Parke, MBE (1884-1974)

R A Parke probably became a member of Trinity congregation in 1904. It was on 29 February of that year that he joined the staff of the Tyrone Constitution as a reporter. Ten years later he was appointed Editor, a post that he retained for 55 years until his retirement in 1969 at the age of 85. R A Parke was a member of the Church Committee from 1938 until 1958. For many years he was the father figure of Unionism in Tyrone and Mid-Ulster. He was also a life-long member of Omagh YMCA, where he was a former Secretary and President. Mr Parke's brother, James, died in the Great War 1914-18 and is remembered on the War Memorial at the back of Trinity Church. R A Parke's son, the late Robert (Bertie) Parke, was both Secretary and Treasurer of the Church.

Roberts M Dale (c 1886-1936)

Roberts Dale was a member of the Church Committee from 1914 and an Elder from 1923 until his death. He succeeded his father in the family hardware and grocery business in John Street. He lived at 24 John Street. Roberts was a very intelligent man with a keen interest in astronomy, on which he frequently gave lectures. He was well read and informed and possessed a very broad outlook on life. Everything that savoured of bigotry or intolerance was foreign to his disposition. He had a clear grasp of the Bible and a steadfast faith. This was reflected in his work for the Church and also through his services to Christian Endeavour, where he was Omagh Branch Treasurer, and Omagh YMCA, where he was a founder member and an Honorary Secretary for 15 years. He had two brothers who went on to become Ministers of religion. Sadly, he died from blood poisoning at the age of 50, after pricking a finger on a protruding nail in a tea-chest. In fond memory of him the following poem was written and published by Mrs H M Price, a well-known local poet of the day.

Roberts Mussen Dale

A friend is taken from our side,
No more in life to see,
No more can we in him confide
Whate'er our troubles be,
A friend who proved himself sincere,
A brother kind and true'
A man whose words of hope and cheer,
Brought strength and courage new.

We miss him in the church, where we
His faithfulness recall,
A member who was proud to be
The strengthener of all.
To him the Sabbath day of rest
Was set apart for God,
And so throughout the week, his best
Was still to Him outpoured.

We miss him at his daily work,
His vacant place we see,
The tasks he never tried to shirk
Were done so faithfully.
He followed in the steps of Him
Whose feet life's pathway trod,
Through sunshine and through shadows dim,
The road that leads to God.

Now he is gone to meet the King
He worshipped and adored,
Death can no longer terror bring,
Nor mystery afford.
We lose a friend sincere and true,
The parting's full of pain,
Whilst days or years that pass are few
Till we shall meet again.

H.M. PRICE
3/9/36

Thomas J Cathcart (1887-1947)

Thomas Cathcart was Clerk of Session from 1945 until his death in 1947. He was a member of the Church Committee for 20 years and an Elder for 13 years. His sudden death occurred just before Communion Sunday, and it is reported that he had already prepared and addressed all envelopes for this occasion and left them, ready for dispatch, on his bedside table. At his memorial service Rev Pinkerton stated

I have never met anyone whose thoughtfulness for others was developed to such a high degree. The most casual stranger was regarded as a brother; if he was in any difficulty or need, the helping hand of T J Cathcart was always ready to do what he could. Few congregations have been blessed with such a loyal servant.

Thomas Cathcart was originally from Ballymena. He was Managing Director of J B Anderson and Co Ltd (drapers and house furnishers), Market Street, Omagh. His son, John, was Church Secretary from 1961 to 1977.

John Montgomery (Church Officer, 1916-1932)

John Montgomery was a native of Londonderry who first came to Omagh with his employers, Colhoun (builders). He was a master carpenter/joiner and helped to build the Sacred Heart Church, Tyrone County Hospital, the Sexton's house in John Street and the Church hall. He also did finishing work in the Second Omagh Church following its major extensions in 1901. His excellent workmanship is manifested in all the woodwork of the wards and the windows of the original County Hospital. Following these experiences he decided to settle in Omagh where his talents were in much demand. He served as Church Officer (Sexton) from 1916 until his death in 1932. For this he was paid £9 per annum, but his contract allowed him to rent 40 John Street for 6 pence (2.5 new pence) per month. It is reported that he discharged his duties for the Church with the faithfulness and diligence which were characteristics of his life.

Miss Dorothy Hall (c 1888-1961)

Miss Hall was a member of the Committee of Trinity Church and was also a member of nearly every organisation in connection with the Church. She was the youngest daughter of James and Margaret Hall. Dorothy Hall was a schoolteacher by profession and was, for many years, Principal of Corrickbridge School, the first school in County Tyrone to introduce the school milk scheme and later a school meals service. She lived at 12 Derry Road, Omagh. A coveted Sunday School award, the Teddy Hall Prize, was presented by Miss Hall in memory of her brother. In her last will and testament she left her home and contents to the Women's Home Mission.

A T (Bertie) Duncan (c 1895-1964)

Bertie Duncan was a member of the Church Committee from 1931 and an Elder for 17 years. He was also an officer in First Omagh Company of the Boys' Brigade for many years. He was a farmer who lived at Mossbank, Mountjoy East, Omagh. His farm, on the Gortin Road, included the present site of Greenhill Cemetery. Mr Duncan was prominent in public life as a locally elected member of the Rural Council, as a member of the Unionist Party and as a member of the Orange Order. His nephew, Albert Bell, and his family are present members of Trinity congregation.

Arthur H Coote (1896-1956)

Arthur Coote was a Church Committee member for 28 years, including 22 years as an Elder. He was a native of Clogher, where his family had a manufacturing business. He represented Aughnacloy division on Tyrone County Council before giving up public life to become Accountant to Tyrone County Council. He came to live in Omagh about 1928, when he joined Trinity congregation - a decision prompted, no doubt, by his landlady at that time, Mrs Barr of 10 Holmview Terrace, who was herself a Trinity stalwart.

Mr Coote was promoted to the post of Secretary of the County Council in 1938, but before that he agreed to accept the temporary post of Treasurer to the congregation in 1932 during the illness of the post-holder, Mr Swan. He remained as Church Treasurer for 23 years. In his first year of office he made a point of visiting non-attenders and non-payers and reported this at the annual meeting, ending by saying, "I feel sure that some non-subscribing members have become reformed Presbyterians."Arthur Coote's father, William, was a Member of Parliament from 1916 to1920, representing the constituency of South Tyrone. His wife, Eileen, was a daughter of Chancellor Dagg, former Rector of Fivemiletown. She was well known in Omagh as the town Librarian and was also very active in the work of Trinity Church. Their daughters (Jean and Margaret) are current members of the congregation.

Joseph Crawford (c 1902-1972)

Joseph Crawford was Clerk of Session of Trinity Church from 1958 to 1971. He was a member of the Church Committee for 44 years, including 38 years as an Elder. With his uncle, also named Joseph, he opened Messrs Crawford and Crawford's shop at Market Street, Omagh and later became sole proprietor.

R S Monteith (1905-1969)

R S (Bertie) Monteith was an Elder in Trinity for 36 years. He was an active member of the Church Committee and was Congregational Secretary from 1928 until 1938. He was associated with the Sabbath School for more than 50 years, first as a pupil, then as a teacher and for 35 years as Superintendent. Bertie Monteith also had a long link with the Boys' Brigade Company, rising through the ranks to become its captain. He lived first at Coneywarren and then at Dunard, 35 Dublin Road, Omagh. He was Managing Director in the retail shoe firm of Swan and Mitchell, where he was a lifetime employee. His wife, Mattie, who predeceased him by two years, was also prominent in Trinity Church life. She was a gifted singer and a key member of the Church choir. Bertie's father, Robert, was also a member of the Church Committee, from 1902 to 1912.

Robert Parke (1913-1993)

Robert (Bertie) Parke was a lifelong member of Trinity Church. He was a solicitor who served for many years as Secretary of Tyrone County Council, where he was regarded as one of the most able and efficient administrators in local government. He joined his father as a member of the Church Committee in 1945 and in the same year became its Secretary, a post that he held for 10 years until he was elected Congregational Treasurer, in which office he remained for a further 12 years. He was highly respected throughout the Presbyterian Church in Ireland and provided wise counsel to Trinity Committee for more than 40 years. Like his father, he was a long- time member of Omagh YMCA and a former Secretary. He was a talented gardener and had frequent successes at the local Horticultural Society's annual shows.

His widow, Mrs Olive Parke, and son Gregory and family are current members of the congregation. Gregory is a member of the Church Committee.

John A Cathcart (1916-1981)

John Cathcart served on the Church Committee for 33 years. He was an Elder for 25 years and Congregational Secretary from 1961 to 1977. He was one of the best-known businessmen in Omagh, being Managing Director of J B Anderson and Co Ltd, Market Street, since 1947, when he succeeded his father, Mr T J Cathcart. John was an excellent organiser and administrator. He was widely known and popular in the community, where he was actively involved in many organisations. He took an active and keen interest in all the affairs of the Church and was a good friend and adviser to many. The seats in the Church choir were donated by John's widow, Mrs Florence Cathcart, in his memory. Mrs Cathcart is a current member of the congregation.

Samuel (Barney) Maguire (Church Officer, 1932-1964)

Samuel (Barney) Maguire was Church Sexton from 1932 until 1964. Barney came from Ballybay in County Monaghan. He was a Sergeant and Drill Instructor in the Royal Irish Fusiliers and served in both North and South of Ireland as well as in India and other places. When stationed in Omagh he lived first in Castle Street and then at Coneywarren . It was during Dr Gibson's ministry that Barney accepted the part-time job as Sexton and moved, with the family, into residence at 40 John Street. At that time he had a full-time position as porter with the Provincial Bank in High Street, Omagh. He had a very strict upbringing, with Lord's Day observance central to family life.

During Barney's time at Trinity there was a hedge around the Church, and the Wee Johnny Room was above the Sexton's living-room but was entered from the balcony in the Church hall. During his first few years the church boiler was lit at 4.00 am each Sunday with turf and fir cones, the fire being sustained with coke purchased from the town gasworks. The church was heated through several grills in each aisle.

Barney Maguire had three sons, who were all given weekly tasks in relation to church upkeep. Sweeping the floors, including pews, was one such task. Every Saturday the brass name-plates on pews and the umbrella stands were polished. On Sunday morning the pavement from 40 John Street round to Fairmount Road was swept by one of the boys.

Barney's job as Sexton lasted for about 32 years, during which time he worked hard with heating systems and other equipment that would be regarded as inefficient and old-fashioned nowadays. During his time the Boys' Brigade was flourishing .He was an Officer and the Drill Instructor for the Company.

Barney's son, Roy Maguire, and his extended family continue the Maguire family connection with Trinity.

William Porter (1921-1990)

William Porter was a lifelong member of Trinity, a member of the Church Committee for 32 years and an Elder for 15 years. He was a most diligent Covenant Treasurer for more than 20 years. William was an estate agent, auctioneer and livestock salesman who was highly successful in business and greatly respected in the Omagh community. Each year he applied his professional skills for the Church's benefit by holding an auction for congregational funds. His wife, Isobel, is an active member of the present congregation, and his son, Alan, is a member of the Church Committee.

The Dick and MacKenzie families

Thomas Dick was a member of Trinity congregation for about 20 years. He lived at Mountjoy Road, Omagh having come from Douglas Bridge. He lived first at Ballynullarty, Newtownstewart. He was a nephew of Rev Robert Dick, who preached for 65 years in Douglas Presbyterian Church. Rev Dick was still preaching at the age of 94, shortly before his death and for several years he was the father of the Presbyterian Church's General Assembly. Thomas was a member of the Church Committee and served as its Honorary Secretary for at least seven years, until 1945. He was senior partner in Messrs Dick and Crawford (estate agents), Market Street, Omagh. He was a member of Tyrone County Council from 1928 to1947 and a member of Omagh Urban Council for 11 years. He was also Chairman of Omagh Regional Education Committee. Thomas Dick's daughter, Jean MacKenzie, was to follow in her father's footsteps in Church and civic life.

Jean married Duncan MacKenzie, who came to Omagh as an agricultural advisor in 1928. They lived at 7 James Street, immediately opposite Trinity Church. At that time Duncan was in charge of horticulture, bee-keeping and forestry in Tyrone, and he was widely known all over the county. He served in World War I with the Royal Army Medical Corps and was in Baghdad and India. Duncan was elected to the Church Committee in 1929 and became an Elder in 1956. He was Choirmaster for many of the 29 years of his choir membership.

Duncan and Jean MacKenzie

Jean MacKenzie was a prominent member of the Ulster Unionist Party and a long- serving member of Omagh District Council. In Church life she was an important member of the strong Trinity branch of the Presbyterian Women's Association for many years. She was also a member of the Church Committee from 1961 until her death in 1981.

Jean and Duncan faced a major tragedy in their lives in March 1958 with the death of their only son, Kenneth, aged 19. Kenneth died of polio while a university student in Belfast. The impact of this, and his parents' love for the Church, is reflected in later gifts and bequests, several to the memory of Kenneth. The Pulpit Fall was donated to Kenneth's memory in 1973, and the two Glastonbury chairs in the Church are in memory of Duncan and Kenneth. Jean MacKenzie also presented the Church with window flower baskets in memory of her parents, Mr and Mrs Thomas Dick, and she bequeathed a generous amount to the Church on her death.

The McCauley family

The McCauley family joined Trinity (or, as it was then, Second Omagh) in 1906. They were previously members of Gillygooley. Mr James McAuley, the head of the household, lived at Cloghog House,Omagh and was a highly respected farmer. His brother, John, lived at Tarlum. John was a batchelor and died in 1897, aged 75. Their sister, Mary Jane was responsible for the erection of the McAuley memorial headstone at the Dublin Road cemetery.

James's arrival at Second Omagh coincided with the baptism of his youngest son, Harold. In all, James and his wife Esther had eight children. They were Sarah Jane, Isaac, Esther, Henrietta, James, Josias, Menzies and Harold. Josias served on the Church Committee for eight years until 1927. He was succeeded by Harold who was later to serve on the Church Committee for 64 years, including six years as Congregational Secretary and 36 years as a ruling Elder. Interestingly, between 1919 and 1928 the spelling of the surname in Church records changed from "McA" to "McC". The reason for this is unknown.

James McAuley Sen. died in 1913 leaving Esther to bring up their eight children. Three of these children became Doctors of Medicine. Menzies was a specialist in Tropical Medicine in Fiji and Esther practiced in England. Esther, later Mrs McMillan, was a great academic who had twenty six letters after her name. Before reading Medicine at Trinity College, Dublin (aged 45), she had also taken teaching and accounting qualifications. She went back to Trinity College at the age of seventy to obtain a law degree. Esther returned to Omagh and Trinity Church in 1983. She died in 1994 aged one hundred.

Dr James McCauley Jun practised in Omagh and in 1944 he lived at Ashdene, Campsie Road. He had six children namely, James, Joy, Nancy, Roy, Joan and Kay. James and Roy followed the family tradition and became doctors, James in Australia and Roy in the United States of America.

McCauley family (Ashdene) c 1956
Back row (l to r): Roy, Joy, Nancy and Jimmy.
Front row: Kay, Mrs Daisy McCauley and Joan

Esther McAuley Sen died in 1948. In 1950 the McCauley family donated two stained glass windows - one at either side of the pulpit. The windows were presented by the family of the late Esther McCauley, at the suggestion of her son, Dr James McCauley Jun, who unfortunately was taken ill with a heart attack within a day or so of his mother's death and passed away six months later. The inscription reads as follows:

"To the Glory of God
and in memory of
a loving Mother
Esther McCauley
1864-1948.
This window is the Gift
of her Grateful Children.
1st October 1950"

Later, in 1969, Mr and Mrs Harold McCauley presented the hymn boards in the church, and in 1977 they presented a lectern chair.

Gertie and Harold McCauley c 1960

In addition to his long and distinguished service to the Church, Harold McCauley was Deputy Director of Education for Tyrone from 1947 to 1953, when he returned to farming. He was also one of the most highly respected businessmen in Omagh, where he owned Messrs Thomas Scarffe and Son Ltd (builders' merchants) and J and R Waterson's (coal merchants), both in Scarffe's Entry before its redevelopment. Harold was also prominent in civic affairs, being Chairman of Omagh District Council in 1975 and also acting on the regional Education and Health Boards, as well as actively supporting the work of several charities, including the Presbyterian Residential Trust, to which he donated land and a substantial sum of money for the establishment of the Harold McCauley Home at Killyclogher Road, Omagh. In 1978 he became the oldest man in Northern Ireland to have undergone coronary by-pass surgery and in 1986 he established the Harold McCauley Fund for Cardiovascular Research. Later a Chair in Opthamology was also established at Queens University, Belfast. On a more light-hearted note, Harold McCauley could always be identified in Church as the person who wore a fresh flower in his buttonhole all the year round.

The McCauley family is currently represented in the Church by Mrs Gertie McCauley and Miss Kay McCauley.

The Todd family

The Todd family came from Corlea, Omagh where Mr RD Todd had a farm. They had 11 children of whom both Herbert and Frederick were later to be Clerks of Session in Trinity Church.

Herbert Todd, son Carl and Carl's wife Jennifer, 2004

Herbert B Todd (Herbie), having considered teaching as a career, opted instead for the post of Office Manager with JB Andersons where he worked for many years before taking up a similar position in Nestles when that firm arrived in Omagh. Herbie was a Sunday School teacher before being elected to the Church Committee in 1936, ordained an Elder in 1956 and he became Clerk of Session from 1972 to 1976. On his retirement in 1976 Herbie and his wife moved to Portadown where their son and daughter lived. He celebrated his 95th birthday earlier in 2004.

Fred and Blanche Todd 1993

Frederick G Todd (Fred) served his time to the grocery and hardware business, first with JR Pollock, High Street, Omagh before going into partnership with Sam Pollock at 19 John Street. Later he worked at Loanes of Kesh and formed another partnership with Willie Johnston at Abbey Street, Omagh before starting his own business at 24 and 26 John Street which he purchased from Mrs Anderson as a going concern (formerly Roberts Dale and Son). Fred married Blanche Nethery, a teacher from Drumquin, and they set up home in Newtownstewart (Moyle House) for a number of years, eventually moving to Knockbeg, Lammy, where their family were born. Ethne, their only daughter was killed in a tragic car accident in London and their two sons, Ronnie and Roy, settled in England. After retirement from business Fred and Blanche moved to a bungalow on the Hospital Road, Omagh, but eventually sold up and moved to England to be near their sons. Fred was elected to the Church Committee in 1957 and became a ruling Elder in 1975. He was Clerk of Session in Trinity from 1980 until 1992. Fred died in 1999. Blanche died in March 2004. Trinity Church had a central place in the lives of Fred and Blanche. The numerous gifts that they bestowed on the Church are recorded elsewhere in this book and remain as permanent testaments to their love and generosity.

Trinity Church Album
1900-1949

Group taken at Omagh Courthouse at the opening of a Bazaar for Trinity Church. Included are: Rev JHR Gibson, Mrs Smyth from Strabane (holding handbag), who opened the Bazaar, John K McConnell (back right), RD Swan (middle right) and other members of the congregation.

Photograph taken during a re-visit by Very Rev Dr Geroge Thompson, who was minister of Trinity Presbyterian Church from 7th April, 1893 to 14th April, 1903. Dr Thompson was Moderator of the General Assembly in 1923.
Standing, left to right: J. Crawford, TJ Cathcart, R Dale, TJ McAdam, HM McCauley, Miss McKnight, Miss M McCandless, Mrs J Wilson, J Wilson, RS Monteith, RD Swan, J McConkey. Seated, left to right: Mrs G Thompson, Very Rev Dr George Thompson, Dr JHR Gibson, Mrs JHR Gibson

Mr and Mrs Robert Monteith with son Bertie 1906

Joseph Crawford Sen. c 1910

Misses Ethel and Minnie McCandless c 1929

This ladies outing in 1937 includes Mrs Mattie Monteith (left) and Denise White (right)

Davy Young, who was a well known character in Omagh. He had a 'sweet shop' in High Street and he organised excursions

Dr JE McCauley c 1946

1950s

Charles and Fanny McFarland, Lammy c 1955.

Herbert Todd, wife Daisy, son Carl and daughter Ann c 1956

Mr and Mrs James Monteith and Raymond 1956

Mr and Mrs Arthur McFarland with Herbie, John and Jill c 1950

Back row: Cecil Hamilton, Kyle Mulligan, Derek Dunne, Campbell Henderson, John Mansell, John Johnson. Third row: Albert Johnston, Carl Logan, Ken McKenzie, Dr H. Mitchell, Harold Monteith, Brian McIvor. Second row: _ Lockard, Mr Monteith (Capt.), Mr Maguire (Officer), Stanley Birrell, _ Short. Front row: Joe McDonald, _, Tom Mansell, _, David Collins, Robbie Barbour.

Mr and Mrs Bertie Monteith with Anne and Harold 1950s

The Pinkerton family c 1954

Rev and Mrs Pinkerton having been presented with two TV chairs

Mr and Mrs Robert Mitchell c 1950

Mr and Mrs David Orr with Betty, Ronnie and Georgie c 1950

Mr and Mrs JA Cathcart, Mr and Mrs RS Monteith and Anne Monteith attending a wedding at Trinity Church c 1955.

1960s

The Armstrong family 1969
William and Jeannie Armstrong were married in Trinity
Church on 27 August 1919. This photograph of them with
their children was taken in 1969 on their Golden Wedding
anniversary. Back Row (L to R): Hettie, Claire, Enid, Mavis.
Front Row: Florence, Nancy, Dolly, William and Jeannie,
Sammy and Audrey.

The McGrew family 1964
Mrs Isabella McGrew (front) with her 8 children
Standing: (L to R) Sam, Jack, Sadie, Joe, Leslie, Willie.
Seated: May and Annabel.

Mrs Simpson (organist) leaving Church

The Mullin family c 1967. George and Anna Mullin with
Barbara and Kenneth

The Crawford family 1967
Mr and Mrs Joseph Crawford (back row-right), their
daughter Stella, daughter-in-law Aileen and grandchildren.
Back row (l to r): Anthony Crawford, Stella Cathcart, Aileen
Crawford, Emma Crawford, Joseph Crawford. Middle: Peter
Crawford. Front row: Jeremy Crawford, Malcolm Cathcart,
Frazer Cathcart, Fiona Cathcart.

Alan, Ruth and Elizabeth Porter c 1964

1970-1989

The Carson family c 1980.
L to r: Georgina (Browne), Sally
(Evans), Betty (Buchanan), Mrs
Elizabeth Carson and Tommy.

Group present at the licensing of Charles McMullen. L to R: W Givens, Fred
Todd, Rev RWW Clarke, Rev B Hunt, Charles McMullen, Rev N McCormick, J
McCarroll, Rev JF Murdoch, JI Gervais, RA Black

Mr and Mrs Jamie Millar 1985

Mr and Mrs Noel Logan with Andrew,
Craig and Jeffrey.

Mr and Mrs WH Johnston

Sponsored walk c 1987

David and Joan Gibson
Church Officers

The Clarke family 1972

Mrs Colvin and Miss Renee McKee who attended Trinity Church before moving
to live in Mountfield. They were sisters and the proprietors of a very successful
bakery and café business trading as The Cake Shop in Market Street, Omagh

1990s

Agnes and Colin Knox

Group at Rev RWW Clarke's retirement. L to R: Betty Gallagher, Sam Gallagher, Mavis Jardine, Arthur McGale, Mrs A Clarke, Stephen Beattie, Blanche Todd, Fred Todd, Rev RWW Clarke, Rev Charles McMullen, Mrs McMullen, Jonathan McNally, Tommy Strain and Rev Brian Hunt.

Mr and Mrs Andy Aiken 1999

Kenneth and Maureen Allen with (l to r), Philip, Karen and Stephen.1998

The Herron family arrive in Omagh. 1993

The Jardine 'brigaders' c 1992

21st Century

Albert Bell presents daughter Kim with her Brigader Brooch. 2003

Rev and Mrs Rick Brand with Rev and Mrs Herron 2002

Heralding the way! Dawn McClung giving the 'Herald' to Mrs May Baillie. 2004

Lorraine McFarland receiving a presentation from Rev Herron.2004

Rev and Mrs RWW Clarke 2003

John Moore and Rev RWW Clarke 2003

Mina McFarland Church Officer

Church Office Bearers

THE Church has assembled as much information as has been possible about its past office bearers. All recorded Clerks of Session, Congregational Secretaries, Church Treasurers and Sunday School Superintendents are listed below.

CLERKS OF SESSION

		inc	
Greer	James	1856	
McAdam	Thomas J.	1890	1942
Cathcart	Thomas J.	1942	1947
Crawford	Joseph	1947	1972
Todd	Herbert B.	1972	1976
McFarland	Arthur	1976	1980
Todd	Frederick W.	1980	1992
Gallagher	Samuel J.	1992	

T. J. McAdam

Thomas J. Cathcart

Joseph Crawford

Herbert Todd

Arthur McFarland

Fred Todd

Samuel Gallagher

CONGREGATIONAL SECRETARIES

McKnight	William J.	Bef 1856	Inc. 1867
Ferguson	Robert	Inc. 1879	
Ferguson	Armer J.	Inc. 1885	1893
McAdam	Thomas J.	1893	1897
Dale	William	1897	1903
McConnell	John Knox	1903	1928
Monteith	Robert S.	1928	1938
Dick	Thomas J.	1938	1945
Parke	Robert	1945	1955
McCauley	Harold S.	1955	1961
Cathcart	John A.	1961	1977
Millar	WJ A	1977	1984
McCandless	John W.	1985	

TJ McAdam

William Dale

John K McConnell

RS Monteith

Robert (Bertie) Parke

Harold McCauley

John A Cathcart

WJA Millar

John McCandless

CHURCH TREASURERS

		Bef.	inc
Houston	John	1856	1867
		Bef.	
Kirk	Hugh Robert	A1894	1914
Swan	Douglas	1914	1932
Coote	Arthur H.	1932	1955
Parke	Robert	1955	1967
Elliott	Robert A.	1967	1972
McKeeman	Archibald	1972	1974
Johnston	Thomas J.	1975	1978
McCandless	John W.	1979	1981
Donald	Noel	1982	1987
Duffield	Derek	1988	1991
Keys	W.Ronald	1992	

Douglas Swan

Arthur H Coote

Robert Parke

Robert A. Elliott

Archibald McKeeman

Thomas J. Johnston

John W. MCandless

Noel Donald

Derek Duffield

W. Ronald Keys

The fullest possible details of all former Elders and committee representatives are listed in **APPENDIX 4**. Photographs of many past members are included in the following pages.

ELDERS

T C Dickie

Joseph Anderson

T J McAdam

R D Swan

William Dale

Roberts Dale

J J McConkey

Joseph Crawford

T J Cathcart

R S Monteith

Arthur W McFarland

Arthur Coote

Bertie Duncan

Joseph Crawford Senior

Arthur McFarland

David Orr Senior

Duncan MacKenzie

Edgar Weir

Harold McCauley

Herbert Todd

J C White

John A Cathcart

Norman McClure

W Martin

Dr Samuel Gilmour

Fred Todd

Ivan Stevenson

Noel Logan

W H Johnston

William Coote

William Porter

WS Mitchell

Andrew Thompson

WJA Millar

James McMullen

M Cuthbertson

ORDINATION OF ELDERS 1972 L to R: (back row)W Mitchell, Rev McIlroy, Rev H Pinkerton, Rev K Gregg, Rev RWW Clarke, Rev Boyd Moore, Rev JF Murdoch, Noel Logan. **Front:** *Fred Todd, A Thompson, W Porter, R Orr, Dr S Gilmour and W Coote.*

ORDINATION OF ELDERS 1995 L to R: *S Hammond, Rev A Rankin, Rev JF Murdoch, Rev I Mairs, S Gallagher, Bill King.* **FRONT:** *D Duffield, R Keys, J McCay, Rev Robert Herron, Mrs J Cummins, A McFarland and J Moore.*

Rev Clarke and some Elders 1991. L to R: *(back) N Donald, R Orr, RA Elliott, RS McCay, and SC Graham.*
FRONT: F Todd, S Gallagher, Rev RWW Clarke, Miss G Cuthbertson and C Jardine.

The Moderator visits Trinity 1992 L to R: *R Orr, S Gallagher, RA Elliott, Rev I Mairs, C Jardine, JD Black, F Todd, Rev*
Dr John Dunlop, Moderator of the General Assembly, SC Graham, Uel Knox, Miss G Cuthbertson, RS McCay, W Coote, JW
McCandless, N Donald, J McMullen.

ORDINATION OF ELDERS 1990 FRONT L to R: S Gallagher, J McMullen, Uel Knox, Rev RWW Clarke, Miss G Cuthbertson, C Jardine and RS McCay. **BACK:** Rev JF Murdoch, Rev A O'Neill, Rev J Braithwaite, W Coote, B Black, F Todd, J Hogg, J Todd, J McCrory, M Cuthbertson, Rev B McManus

COMMITTEE MEMBERS

King Houston

H McFadden

W Houston

Joseph Wilson

Capt John B Anderson

J F Dickie

David Black

Robert Mitchell

Robert Monteith

Mrs Barr

A F Colhoun

R A Parke

W Mc Galliard

W R Dick

W J Moore DFC

Arthur Simpson

Douglas Chambers

Fred McCloskey

Nora J McAdam

Dr J Moore Johnston

Herbert Moore

Jim Gourley

J P Graham

Ronnie McDermott

John Wallace	John Gordon	Jean MacKenzie	Archie Burton
Bertie Forsythe	James Kincaid	Mrs May McFarland	Samuel McConnell
William C Hamilton	George Mullin	William Browne	Samuel Perkins
Robinson Stewart	Robert Chisholm	Neil Gilmour	Nat Maginnis

Kenneth McConnell

George Dunne

Hamilton Baxter

Andrew Aiken

Mrs A Clarke

David McIlwaine

Ministers

Adapted from "A History of Congregations in the Presbyterian Church in Ireland 1610-1982" Published by Presbyterian Historical Society. Robert Knox Buick.

The Church's first two Ministers, Rev Robert Nelson and Rev David Gilkey, served the congregation for almost 100 years. Rev Robert Nelson was a Tyrone man, a son of William Nelson, Urney. He was licensed in Letterkenny Presbytery and ordained here in July 1754. He continued an active ministry till he passed away on 8 April 1801. He received his education at Glasgow University, as did his successor, Rev David Gilkey, a native of Glendermott and son of Andrew, a farmer. Mr Gilkey was ordained on 3 February 1803. His ministry lasted 38 years, but towards the end the strength of the congregation declined "owing to their minister's interpretation of Church principles being too elastic for their tastes." Mr Gilkey retired in 1841 and died on 15 May 1850.

On 2 February 1842 **Rev Josias Mitchell**, born in Newbliss, County Monaghan, was ordained as assistant and successor to Rev David Gilkey. It was during his ministry that the present church was built on the same site as the one erected in the year 1752.

Rev Mitchell retired on 16 December 1879, when his assistant and successor, Rev Thomas Hamill, was ordained. Mr Mitchell passed away in July 1882. Three of his daughters married clergymen - Rev J C Clarke, DD, Rev George McFarland, BA and Rev Samuel Paul.

Rev Thomas McAfee Hamill, MA, born on 30 March 1853, was the son of James Hamill, Ballymoney. He was licensed at Route Presbytery on 6 May 1879 and was installed as Minister of Second Omagh later that year. From Second Omagh he was called to Lurgan on 12 February 1884 and was later appointed Professor of Systematic Theology in the Presbyterian College, Belfast (1895-1919) and Moderator of the General Assembly (1915-1916). He died on 17 February 1919.

Mr Hamill was succeeded in Omagh by **Rev William Johnston, BA**. Mr Johnston was the son of James Johnston, Burren, Ballynahinch. He was licensed at Down Presbytery on 29 April 1883 and was ordained on 30 September 1884. Mr Johnston remained in Omagh for exactly three years, when he moved to Wolverhampton. He died on 10 January 1945.

His successor, **Rev James Alexander Campbell, MA**, born on 13 November 1858, was the son of James Campbell, Ballinasloe. Educated at Queen's College, Galway, he was licensed at Athlone on 7 August 1883 and came to Second Omagh from Stewartstown. He was installed on 27 March 1888 but resigned on 15 April 1890 to become the Minister of Sandymount in Dublin. Later years (1903-1917) were spent in South Africa, followed by two years in Liverpool. Mr Campbell died on 4 September 1919.

Rev Robert Wallace, born in 1845, son of Robert, Castleblayney, and licensed at Newry Presbytery on 5 June 1869, was ordained on 3 July 1890. He had been the Minister of Ballygoney from 24 July 1873. Mr Wallace remained until his death on 20 January 1898.

Rev George Thompson, born in Eglinton and educated at Magee College, was licensed at Glendermott in 1880. Mr Thompson - later to have DD added to his name - having been Minister of Newtowncunningham, was installed as Minister of Second Omagh on 7 April 1898 and had a very fruitful ministry for five years, ending on 14 April 1903 on his acceptance of a call from Cliftonville, Belfast. Dr Thompson was Joint Convenor of the Foreign Mission in 1909 and followed in the footsteps of an earlier Minister of Second Omagh, Rev Dr T Hamill, to become Moderator of the General Assembly in 1923. He died on 1 September 1946. It was in 1901, during Dr Thompson's ministry, that the church was enlarged by the addition of transepts, entrance porch and Minister's room, which enhanced the architecture of the building.

The next Minister was **Rev W J Baird**, BA. Born on 31 December 1866 at Ardstraw, he was educated at Queen's University, Belfast and was licensed at Strabane Presbytery on 7 May 1890. Previously Minister of Killead, from 16 April 1891, Mr Baird was installed on 30 July 1903 and resigned on 26 July 1904, having accepted a call from the congregation of Agnes Street, Belfast. He resigned from there on 26 July 1932 and died on 3 May 1944.

Mr Baird was succeeded in Second Omagh by **Rev H W Morrow, MA**, who was born on 11 December 1857, son of William, Magherascouse, Ballygowan.

Mr Morrow was educated at Queen's College, Galway and Queen's University, Belfast. Licensed at Comber Presbytery on 26 May 1884, he was Minister of First Markethill until October 1904. He was installed in Second Omagh on 16 November 1904. Much efficiency marked his work as Pastor of the Omagh Church. He was also an assiduous student and received a DD in 1919. Dr Morrow published three volumes of sermons. It was during his ministry that the congregation's name was changed from Second Omagh to Trinity. He resigned on 4 October 1926 and died on 19 October 1934.

Trinity Church congregation, Sunday 21 December 2003

Trinity Church congregation (Right Transept), Sunday 21 December 2003

Trinity Church congregation (Left Transept), Sunday 21 December 2003

154th Trinity Girls Brigade Company 2004
Back Row (L to R)*:* Sarah McKinley, Lauren Alexander, Jolene Bell, Ruth McQuade, Danielle Barton, Paula Henry.
Middle Row*:* Mavis Jardine (Captain), Mrs Joan Cummins (Inspecting Officer).
Front Row*:* Grace Monteith, Nadine McFarland, Hannah Leonard, Janice McKinley and Melissa Rutledge.

1st Omagh BB Company 2004
Front Row (l to r)*:* Deane Kane, Scott McAleer, John Kerr, Steve Wright, James Kerr
2nd Row*:* Mrs Isobel Bell, Mark Clements, James Rutledge, Simon Thompson, Justin Aiken, Reece Kane, Rev JF Murdoch, Jack Hill, Ben Hall, Stuart Thompson, Matthew Donaldson, Andrew Monteith, Mrs Mandy Milligan.
3rd Row*:* Matthew McKernan, Jack Swann, William Barton, Luke Taylor, Craig Breen, Gary Donaldson, Lloyd Kane, Duncan Wright, Jonathan Agnew
4th Row*:* Marcus Donaldson, Lee Nesbitt, Clive Sproule, Mathew Taylor, Jason Sproule, Mark Wright, Stuart Graham, Ethan Kane, William Hamilton, David Long, Darryl Gilchrist
5th Row*:* Stuart McFarland, Jaymie Hill, David Crawford, Richard Barton, Adam Leitch, Daryl Graham, Richard Bell, Richard Clements, Victor Barton, Matthew Alexander
Back Row*:* Mr Alan Duff, Mrs Valerie Alexander, Ms Dorothy Henry, Ashley Graham, Stephen McConnell, Simon Graham, James Marshall, Iain Herron, John Graham, Andrew Young, Adam Henry, , Mr Drew Hamilton, Mr David Marshall, Mr Noel Barton
Not in photograph*:*
Chaplain*:* Rev R Herron; ***Company Section****:* Malcolm Herron, Matthew Lee; ***Junior Section****:* Paul Strain

Trinity Choir members in their new robes (1984)
Also included are Rev RWW Clarke, Fred and Blanche Todd and David Gibson (Sexton)

Trinity Church Choir Sunday 21 December 2003

Members of Trinity Church Session and Committee 2004
Front Row (L to R): Rev R Herron, Rev RWW Clarke (Senior Minister), WJA Millar (Former Elder and Church Sec.), Pearl Donnell, Claire McElhinney, Joan Cummins, Herbie Todd (Clerk of Session 1972-74), Gladys Cuthbertson, John McCandless, Desmond Black, Ian Leitch.
Second Row (L to R): Derek Duffield, Alfie Sayers, Kenneth Allen, Bob Elliott, Colin Jardine, Jim Adams, Artie McFarland, Uel Knox.
Third Row (L to R): Charles Graham, Raymond Monteith, Ronnie Keys, Robert McCay, Derek Gilmore, Gary Milligan, John McCay.
Back Row (L to R): Samuel Carson, Ronnie Orr, Samuel Gallagher, John Moore, Noel Donald, Alan Porter and Alan Browne.

Trinity Bible Class 2004
Front Row (l to r): Melissa Smyth, Lyndsey McCay, Rebecca McConnell, Jonathan McClung
Middle Row: Sarah Jayne McClung, Richard Gibson, James McCay
Back Row: Richard Armstrong, Malcolm Herron and Keith McKnight

Trinity Presbyterian Womens' Association 2003

Back Row (L to R): *Dorothy King, Beverly Fleming, Audrey McConnell, Mavis Jardine, Rebecca Scott, Heather Campbell, Heather Carson, Gertie Shortt.*
Middle Row: *Joan Cummins, Olive Parke, Ellen McConnell, Irene Knox, , Ann Clarke, Betty Gaston, Eileen Fleming, Margaret Broome, Jean Creery, Edith Hemphill, Olive Moore, Sharon Beattie, Irene McCauley, Annette Moore.*
Front Row: *Bertha Hamilton, Sadie Clements, Alice Clarke, Sheena Herron, Mary Pinkerton, Florence Cathcart, Isobel Porter, Jean McCay and Peggy Gilmore.*

Some of the children of Trinity Sunday School 2004

Front Row (L to R): Katie Buchanan, Emily Buchanan, Ben Somerville, Stephen Armstrong, Kyle Beattie, James Kerr, Matthew Allen, Hannah Graham, Jade Somerville.

Middle Row: Joachim Smyth, Aaron Carson, Lindsay Carson, Grace Monteith, Courtney Allen, Gemma Armstrong, Julie Parke, Kirstin Duncan, Naomi Duncan.

Back Row: Matthew Alexander, Rachael Graham, Katie McCay, Alison Parke and Gemma Beattie

Trinity Presbyterian Church, Omagh (2004)

Rev J H R Gibson, MA, son of Rev John Gibson, Annahilt, was educated at Magee College and Trinity College, Dublin. He was licensed at Ballymena Presbytery in 1915 and was ordained at Granshaw, County Down on 19 April 1916. From Granshaw Mr Gibson was installed at Trinity on 9 February 1927. When Rev S Anderson, Drumlegagh, who had charge of Gillygooley congregation, accepted a call to Granshaw, the congregation of Gillygooley was put under the care of Rev Gibson in September 1928.

Rev Gibson's abilities as an organiser, his diligence and his enthusiasm for the Church's aims and ideals led to his appointment to the position of General Secretary of the Presbyterian Church in Ireland in 1942. He received a DD from Trinity College, Dublin in 1943 and, in 1950, was chosen as Moderator of the General Assembly, the third former Minister of Trinity to achieve this honour in the space of 35 years.

Group outside Trinity Church on the occasion of presentation of Moderatorial robes to Rev Dr JHR Gibson. Front row (L to R) Mrs Erskine, Miss Buchanan, Rev Dr Gibson, Mrs Wilson and Mrs Gibson.. Back row: Rev SEM Brown (Granshaw), Rev WN Maxwell (Woodvale), Mr J Wilson, Rev Dr DG Erskine, Moderator of the General Assembly, Mr TH Barr (Belfast Presbytery), Rev JH Withers (Fisherwick) and Rev RH Pinkerton.

Rev R H Pinkerton, BA of Muckamore Presbyterian Church, County Antrim, and a native of Armagh, came to Omagh with the enthusiasm and vigour of youth to take up the work of Pastor and Teacher that had been faithfully continued by earnest men for almost two centuries. He was installed as Minister of Trinity on 27 January 1943 and was also given charge of Gillygooley Church. The congregation of Gillygooley wholeheartedly decided to continue with the same arrangement whereby the Minister of Trinity also served Gillygooley.

During Rev Pinkerton's years as Minister, extensive repairs and renovation work were carried out to both churches. In Trinity, memorials in the form of plaques, stained glass windows, a pipe organ and a Communion Table added tradition and beauty.

Rev Dr J H R Gibson returned to take part in the unveiling and dedication of windows and the Communion Table. In 1952, to mark its bicentenary, the church was refurbished with carpets and cushions.

In 1957 a major extension to the Church Hall was completed by voluntary labour.

Professor RJ Wilson, Moderator of the General Assembly opening the door of the new hall extension. Included are (l to r) Rev RH Pinkerton, Rev Dr JHR Gibson and Rev JM McAuley, Moderator of Omagh Presbytery.

In June 1970 Mr Pinkerton was installed as Minister of Edenderry Presbyterian Church, thus ending another chapter in the history of Trinity.

Mr Pinkerton was succeeded by the **Rev RWW Clarke, MA,** who came to Trinity from Dundalk and was installed on 12 May 1971. Mr Clarke was the first occupant of the new manse, which was completed in 1973 shortly after his arrival. He was a popular Minister both within Trinity and in the wider Omagh community. During his ministry a further extension to the Church hall was planned and completed, the organ was fully restored, and he was largely responsible for promoting the healing ministry in Omagh Presbytery. Rev Clarke retired in 1992.

Rev RH Pinkerton, Rev Dr JHR Gibson (Clerk to the General Asembly) and Rev RWW Clarke. All three served with distinction as Ministers of Trinity.

Rev Clarke was succeeded by **Rev Robert Herron**, the current Minister. He was installed in May 1993. Mr Herron's previous ministry had been in Strabane, County Tyrone. Under his leadership and ministry, Trinity's Church services have been gradually reshaped and modernised. Mr Herron has also been a prominent figure in the post-Omagh-bomb period, bringing a message of reconciliation, co-operation and hope to the local community.

Other Ministers from Trinity, Omagh

Over its history Second Omagh/Trinity Church has rejoiced to see quite a few former members of the congregation becoming Ministers in the wider Church. These include:

Rev W T Dale (c 1916), Rev David Dale (c 1920)

Rev A W Anderson (c 1920-60)   Rev C G McKnight (c 1944)   Rev Charles Mc Mullen (c 1980)

Ministers who served in Trinity

Nelson, Robert : July 1754 - April 1801

Gilkey, David : February 1803 - 1841

Mitchell, Josias : February 1842 - December 1879

Hamill, Thomas McAfee : December 1879 - February 1884

Johnston, William : September 1884 - September 1887

Campbell, James Alexander : March 1888 - April 1890

Wallace, Robert : July 1890 - January 1898

Thompson, George : April 1898 - April 1903

Baird, William James : July 1903 - July 1904

Morrow, Henry William : November 1904 - October 1926

Gibson, Joseph Hugh Rush : February 1927 - August 1942

Pinkerton, Robert Harold : January 1943 - June 1970

Clarke, Robert William Wylie : May 1971 - April 1992

Herron, Robert : May 1993 - present

The Gillygooley connection

Gillygooley Presbyterian Church

THE congregations of Gillygooley and Second Omagh/Trinity have always been good neighbours. Our members live side by side in the countryside around Omagh and many have relations in both churches. However the first official connection that Trinity Church had with Gillygooley Church was in September 1928, when the Union Commission put Gillygooley under the care of Rev J H R Gibson, then Minister at Trinity. This happy arrangement continued until the two churches were officially united on 1 October 1970.

Interestingly, Rev Gibson had come to Trinity from Granshaw congregation in February 1927. His position at Granshaw was subsequently filled by Rev S Anderson, Drumlegagh, who, although in the Strabane Presbytery had supplied the congregation of Gillygooley from 1922.

Church records also reveal that, even before 1928, the two Churches always had a good relationship. Gillygooley's Minister from 1869 to 1904, Rev Samuel Paul, took Trinity under his wing from January 1898 to March 1898, when it was 'between Ministers'. The ladies of both congregations came together in one PWA. There are regular shared services, and the business end of Church life has always been harmonious.

When Trinity developed its new manse in 1972 the members of Gillygooley congregation contributed £500 towards soft furnishings. A similar gesture was made when the manse was renovated in 1993. The two Churches also publish a common quarterly news-letter, 'Trinity and Gillygooley News'.

The Church memorials

Contributed by Dr Ian Leitch

THE history of Church buildings is often contained within their walls, in the form of memorials, plaques, inscriptions and other memorabilia. Trinity Church, Omagh is no exception. Within its walls there is a wide range of items that reflect the Church's long history and remember some of the people who contributed to its well-being over its lifetime. This section highlights these memorials and, where possible, expands on the information available about each item.

The vestibule

On entering the front porch or vestibule of the Church, the worshippers are greeted by a large blue wooden-framed plaque. It charts chronologically the history of the Church and its buildings, renovations and Ministers from its origins in 1752 to the installation of Rev Robert Herron in 1993. The details on this plaque replace unique carved records previously on window-sills in the Church, which were erroneously destroyed during the renovations in 1969. It is also interesting to note that the arch into which the blue notice board is set is the former main doorway into the church.

Vestibule (front entrance) to Trinity Presbyterian Church.

Visitors standing in front of the large blue plaque will notice a polished wood and glass case on the table before them. It holds several books written by Rev Dr H W Morrow during his ministry at Trinity in the early part of the twentieth century. One of the volumes, entitled "War and Immortality", refers directly to actions during the Great War, which had just passed and which must have had a terrible impact on families of the district.

The oak carved cabinet at the rear wall of the vestibule was presented to the Church in April 1978 in very sad circumstances. It commemorates the late Miss Ethne Todd, only daughter of Fred Todd, Elder and Clerk of Session from 1975 to 1991, and his wife, Blanche. Ethne was killed in a road traffic accident in England. The memorial cabinet was carved by James McGoldrick from an oak beam taken from an old balcony that had been removed from the Church hall.

A small brass plaque in the vestibule reminds visitors of the origins of the Church bell, a central feature of the Church, which rings out every Sunday morning. (See page 20.)

The more observant visitor may notice two large wooden boxes on one of the window-sills. These have slits in the top, rather like modern-day ballot-boxes, and one of them is inscribed 'Sustentation Fund Box'.

Those interested in Church antiquities may admire the two old copper collecting spoons with long wooden handles.

The Buchanan organ

At a service in June 1940 Rev J McIlrath dedicated the new memorial pipe organ. Described in the press as a magnificent gift, it was a fitting memorial to Lieutenant-Colonel Andrew Buchanan and his wife, Mary Kyd Buchanan.

Lieutenant-Colonel Buchanan was born in Killyclogher, Omagh in 1861. A graduate of Queen's University medical school, he had a successful 20-year career as a civil surgeon with the Indian medical service, practising in the central provinces until he retired to Guernsey, where he died on 26 March 1939, aged 77 years. Press reports made much of the quality of the organ. The claim that the craftsmanship and materials are as near perfect as possible is given some credibility by the fact that only by 5 April 1992 was the instrument refurbished and rededicated.

The Buchanan organ

The stained-glass windows

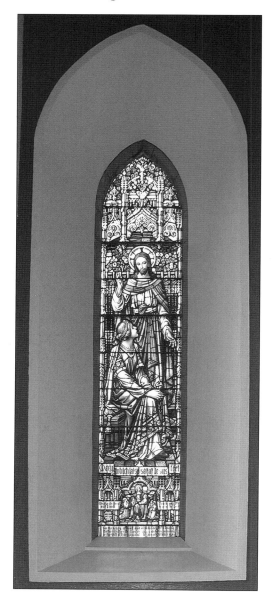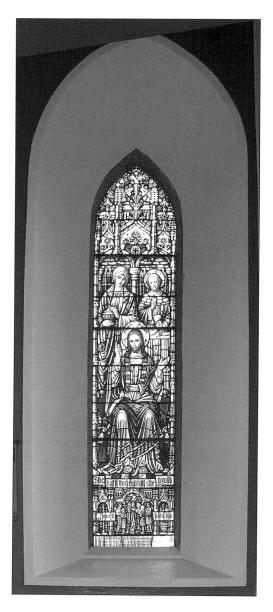

The Esther McCauley memorial windows, in stained glass, stand guard on either side of the pulpit. In the presence of an exceedingly large congregation at the morning service on 1 October 1950, they were unveiled by the wife of the Moderator of the General Assembly, Right Rev Dr J H R Gibson.

The pulpit and choir area

The pulpit fall was donated by Mr and Mrs Duncan MacKenzie in memory of their son, Kenneth, and was dedicated by Very Rev Dr J H R Gibson on 18 March 1973.

Beneath the pulpit fall is a brass plaque indicating that the choir chairs were presented by Florence Cathcart, wife of the late John Cathcart, a ruling Elder and Congregational Secretary for 16 years. The chairs were dedicated on 16 September 1984.

The upright piano situated between the organ and the Communion table was a gift from the late Miss Denise White, a long-time member of the congregation, in memory of her parents, Jack and Sarah Louise White, and was dedicated on 27 November 1988.

At the front right of the choir stall stands the baptismal font, beautifully carved in light oak. It was a gift from Dr Norman H P Crawford on 1 November 1969.

The Psalm boards to the left and right of the pulpit were presented by Mr and Mrs Harold McCauley.

The Bible boards were presented by the Gallagher family in memory of their mother, Eileen, who was a Sunday School Teacher and Organist at Trinity.

On the front surface of the Communion table is a small brass plaque commemorating Thomas J McAdam, a former Congregational Secretary and Clerk of Session, who was "a faithful worshipper and for over 80 years a member of the choir." T J McAdam died on 22 December 1945. A more complete outline of his huge contribution to the Church is given elsewhere in this book.

The offertory plates and brass vase on the Communion table were presented in memory of Raymond Donnell, "a beloved husband and father", by Pearl and Alison, and dedicated on 1 April 1979.

The large Bible on the Communion table was presented by the Cuthbertson family in April 1994.

The velvet Communion Table cover was presented in memory of Robert Nesbitt by Florence, Billy and family.

Four silver Communion plates were donated in 1949 by the daughters of Mr and Mrs James Hall, in memory of Mr and Mrs Hall and their sons, Bobby and Teddy.

The lectern standing to the left of the choir stall was a gift from the wife and daughters of John Pattison (Jack) Graham, a Committee member, who passed away on 25 July 1968.

The lectern fall was presented to the Church by Rev and Mrs RWW Clarke in appreciation of 21 years' happy ministry from May 1971 to April 1992.

The large lectern Bible was presented by Isabel Porter in April 1994 in loving memory of her husband, William Porter, for many years an Elder, who died on 12 August 1990.

The lectern chair was given by Mr and Mrs Harold McCauley on 13 March 1977.

On 3 December 1969, on the reopening of the Church, a lectern Bible was presented by Mr and Mrs Ivan Stevenson.

The robes worn each Sunday by the choir members and a gown for the Sexton were donated by Fred and Blanche Todd on 7 May 1989 (see photo p150).

Right wall of the church

The 22nd September 1985 saw the unveiling of a brass plaque in memory of Rev R H Pinkerton, who served the Church as Minister from 1943 to 1971. A jolly man, he had a tremendous ability to relate to old and young alike. Many in the congregation will recall, as children, eagerly waiting for the 'Wee Johnny' stories that he told each Sunday morning. Following retirement from Trinity and Gillygooley, he moved the short distance to Edenderry Presbyterian Church, where he continued his ministry until his retirement in 1979. He died on 24 February 1985.

The plaque to Victor John Frackleton Wilson commemorates the loss of one of many in 'the war to end all wars'. A young officer, Second Lieutenant Wilson served in the Royal Inniskilling Fusiliers and died in action in Le Cateau, France on 17 October 1918 at the tender age of 19 years. Victor Wilson was the son of Joseph Wilson, a Church Committee member from 1900 until his death in 1954.

The plaque to Thomas Coulter Dickie, BA, which was erected by his wife and children, commemorates a man who was the Sunday School Superintendent for over 30 years. He died on 28 January 1907 (see biographical notes p46).

The King's Colour hangs on the right wall of the church at the angle of the right transept. Flag of the Fifth Battalion the Royal Inniskilling Fusiliers, it was raised at Omagh in 1914 and saw service in the Great War with the regiment at Gallipoli, Servia, Palestine and France. It was dedicated on 15 May 1921 by Rev D McGranahan.

A drum handed over at the 1st Omagh BB enrolment service Nov 1 1987 is located below this flag.

Left wall of the church

On the left wall of the church, just before the left transept, hangs a drum from the Ninth Royal Inniskilling Fusiliers (Tyrone Volunteers), Thirty-sixth Ulster Division. Presented by the colonel and officers, the drum was carried by a battalion that greatly distinguished itself at Thiepval, Mesines, Ypres, Cambrai, St Quentin and the Lys Valley during the Great War.

Just above the drum hangs the standard of the Royal Air Forces Association (Mid Tyrone branch), which was received for safekeeping by the Minister on 4 September 1975, on which occasion the new standard was dedicated by the Moderator of the Presbytery of the Bounds, Rev K Gregg.

Next within the body of the church hangs a brass memorial to Rev Robert Wallace, Minister of the congregation for seven years. He died on 20 January 1898. A newspaper cutting of the time notes the personal esteem in which he was held, recording that Sir Francis Brady, Bart, County Court Judge, adjourned his court on the day of the funeral "to give the professional gentlemen and others who wished to be present an opportunity of attending."

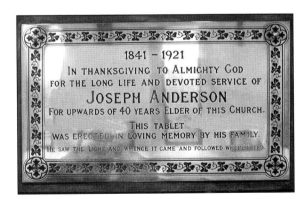

A brass plaque on the left wall of the church bears testament to long life and devoted service. Joseph Anderson (1841-1921) was for 'upwards of forty years' an Elder of the Church. He was highly respected in many walks of Omagh life and was the founder of Messrs J B Anderson. The plaque was erected by his family. A more complete outline of Joseph Anderson's life in the Church and community appears on page 47.

IN EVER GRATEFUL REMEMBRANCE OF
THOSE WHO SERVED IN TWO WORLD WARS
AND OF THOSE WHO LOST THEIR LIVES IN N. IRELAND

1914–1918

THOMAS ALLEN	ROBERT H. C. LYONS
JOHN B. ANDERSON	EILEEN McADAM
MABEL H. B. ANDERSON	THOMAS A. McADAM
ANDREW BUCHANAN	WILLIAM I. McADAM
MAXWELL CHISHOLM	SAMUEL McGREW
ROBERT A. CHRISTIE	JOSEPH McGREW
THOMAS B. CLAY	GEORGE McNICKLE
JAMES COLHOUN	GEORGE MONTGOMERY
JAMES McN. DICKIE	WILLIAM MULLIN
KATHLEEN G. DICKIE	MARGARET MURDOCK
THOMAS C. DICKIE	ROBERT J. PORTER
WALLACE DICKIE	JOSEPH J. TORRENS
MARGUERITE HALL	REBECCA WHITE
MARGARET HAMILTON	JOHN WRAY
WILLIAM KYLE	

FAITHFUL UNTO DEATH

JOHN L. COLHOUN	WILLIAM NIXON
FRANK R. HALL	JAMES PARKE
JOHN A. McADAM	VICTOR JOHN F. WILSON

1939–1945

ELIZABETH ALLEN	JOSEPH McGREW
GEORGE BEATTY	SAMUEL McGREW
ROBERT CHISHOLM	DOROTHY McKILLOP
JIM DUNCAN	THOMAS A. McKILLOP
WILLIAM J. DUNN	MARY MAGUIRE
EDMUND GIBONEY	ROBERT MAGUIRE
GEORGE GIBSON	WILLIAM MAGUIRE
ROBERT GILKENSON	W. J. MOORE
JAMES HALL	JOHN PERKINS
THOMAS A. KANE	GEORGE PORTER
JACK McCOMISKEY	JOHN PORTER
VIVIAN McFARLAND	JOHN WRAY
HENRIETTA ARMSTRONG	

FAITHFUL UNTO DEATH

ROBERT S. CARSON

1969–

JOHN SMITH (R.U.C.)
AUGUST 1981

RONNIE ALEXANDER (U.D.R.)
JULY 1983   GILLYGOOLEY

STEPHEN MONTGOMERY (R.U.C.)
JANUARY 1989

"WE WILL REMEMBER THEM"

A further brass memorial plaque on the left wall records the names of men and women from the congregation who fought in the two world wars, some of whom lost their lives, and three members of the congregation (two RUC personnel, John Smith and Stephen Montgomery, and one UDR member, Ronnie Alexander) who died in the Northern Ireland conflict. Of the 32 who fought in World War I, three died, and one of the 26 who fought in World War II lost his life. This plaque was unveiled on 10 February 1991 by the Chaplain General (Army), Rev Jim Harkness, MA. It is the only church memorial in the Omagh area that commemorates the dead of all the conflicts of the twentieth century.

Rear wall of the church

On the rear wall of the church hangs a marble and brass memorial to six members of the congregation who lost their lives in the Great War. One of the men, Victor John Frackleton Wilson, a Second Lieutenant in the Royal Inniskilling Fusiliers, was killed in France on 17 October 1918 and is commemorated in a separate brass memorial on the right wall.

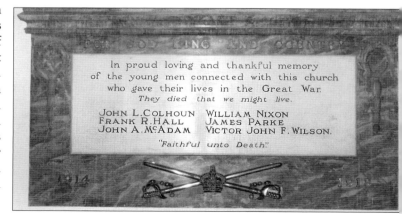

96

GⱽR1

HE whom this scroll commemorates was numbered among those who, at the call of King and Country, left all that was dear to them, endured hardness, faced danger, and finally passed out of the sight of men by the path of duty and self-sacrifice, giving up their own lives that others might live in freedom.

Let those who come after see to it that his name be not forgotten.

Pte. John Leslie Colquhoun Canadian Infantry Bn.

A wooden-framed clock hangs on the rear wall in clear view of the Minister, lest the sermons should overrun. The clock was presented in memory of the late Jim Kincaid "in fond and loving memory of a dear husband and father from wife, son and daughters. May 1991."

Transepts

In the right transept (and mirrored in the left transept) hangs a triangular cupboard for holding Communion ware. These cupboards were presented in tribute to Robert Samuel Monteith, who for 36 years was an Elder of the congregation, Superintendent of the Sunday School and Convenor of the 1969 Church Renovation Committee. He passed away on 9 September 1969.

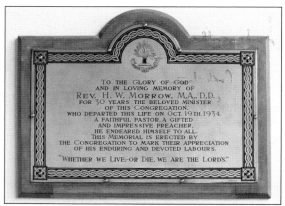

Also in the right transept hangs a tablet in memory of Rev H Morrow, who died on 19 October 1934 after ministering to Trinity for over 30 years. Obviously a scholar, he was a Master of Arts and a Doctor of Divinity. Several of the books he wrote may be found in a presentation box in the vestibule.

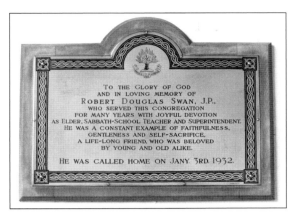

On the wall of the left transept hangs a brass tablet in memory of Robert Douglas Swan JP. A Sunday in 1934 saw the joint unveiling of that memorial and a tablet in memory of Rev Dr H W Morrow.

Robert Douglas Swan was a member of the Church for over 50 years, serving as Elder, Treasurer and Sabbath School Teacher and Superintendent. His obvious love for Trinity was noted in a newspaper article of the time, describing how he visited weekly to ensure that nothing was out of repair. "He took pleasure in its stones. Its very dust to him was dear." The memorial was unveiled by Miss Minnie McCandless, niece of the deceased.

The body of the church

Two Glastonbury chairs (or monks' chairs) adorn the front of the church. They were presented to the congregation by Mrs Jean MacKenzie in memory of her husband, Duncan, who died on 10 February 1977, and their only son, Kenneth, who died on 19 March 1958. They were dedicated on Sunday 22 October 1978 by Rev Moore Wasson of the BBC. The chairs were made by James McGoldrick.

Mrs MacKenzie also presented the Church with window flower baskets in memory of her parents, Mr and Mrs Thomas Dick. Thomas Dick was Congregational Secretary from 1938 to 1945.

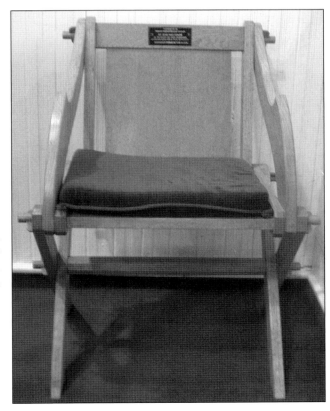

The Church amplification system was presented by an anonymous donor and dedicated on 19 January 1984. It was overhauled and updated in the autumn of 2003 as part of the Church's celebration of its 250th anniversary.

Mr and Mrs Fred Todd donated the Communion linen on 18 March 1973.

Hymn-books for the congregation were presented by the Presbyterian Women's Association (PWA) on 28 December 1975.

The pew Bibles in the church were donated by members of the congregation. Donors are identified by an inscription inside the front cover of each Bible.

The hall

Voluntary labour by the congregation is recognised on the plaque in the foyer of the Church hall. The hall was renovated in 1957, and the extension was opened by the Moderator of the General Assembly, Rt Rev Prof R J Wilson, BA, BD, on 9 October 1957.

 The plaque on the entrance door to the room on the first floor of the hall indicates that it has been named the 'Wee Johnny Room' in tribute to the story-telling acumen of Rev R H Pinkerton.

The children of the Wee Johnny Club are likewise remembered on a wall plaque in the room as providers of the chairs in October 1957. The original chairs have since been replaced by more modern ones.

An electronic organ for choir practice was donated by Mr and Mrs Fred Todd on 10 November 1985.

James McGoldrick is a master craftsman who carved much church furniture in the Omagh area including the Communion table, the Baptismal font, the Todd cabinet and the MacKenzie chairs in Trinity. Here he is making the church bible boards.

Memorials, donations and bequests

In addition to the tangible memorials in the Church buildings, Trinity has benefited through the years from many generous bequests of money, donated usually in memory of former members or Ministers of the congregation. Such contributions are invested, and the income is applied in accordance with the donors' wishes. The list below includes many very dear people who worshipped with us over the years and who were well known and respected by present and previous generations.

Memorials/Donations/Bequests	Purpose
Bequest of late Mrs G. White	Stipend
James & Annie Crawford -Gift	F.W.O
Donation - W. A. Armstrong	F.W.O
Memorial - Miss V Torrens &	
Mr. & Mrs R. Guiver	F.W.O
Memorial - George Mulholland	F.W.O
Memorial - Peggy Ewing	Trinity Youth Council
Memorial - Rev. R. H. Pinkerton	Sabbath school
Investment - Sale of Manse Land	Stipend
MacKenzie Bequest (Sept. 1981	50% Repairs
Valuation £2311.00)	50% Stipend
Bequest - Mrs F.L Bratton	Church Repairs
Bequest of Mrs I.M. White	Stipend
Memorial - Mr. & Mrs. Dunn	Sabbath school
Bequest of late Mrs Barr	Sustentation
Memorial - Mr Joseph Crawford	Sabbath school
Price Bequest	Mission to Lepers
Bequest of late John White	Stipend
Bequest of late Mrs Murphy	Stipend
Memorial - T.C. Dickie	Sabbath school
Bequest of late Miss Eldowney	Stipend
Bequest of late Miss Black	Stipend
Rev. H.W. Morrow	Stipend
Memorial - Teddy Hall	Sabbath school
Bequest of late Neville Elliott	Stipend
Investment - Sale of Manse Land	Stipend
Memorial - Mrs M.J. Mc Farland	Stipend
Memorial - Jack Wilson	Sabbath school
Bequest of late Mrs M.F. Wilson	Stipend
Bequest of late Mrs H.M. Price	P.W.A
Bequest of late Miss M. Graham	Stipend
Bequest - Mr & Mrs Jack White	Church Repairs
R.A. Parke	General Funds
Memorial - W. & J. Elliot	Stipend
Bequest John White	Stipend
Bequest of late Miss Black	CMF
Miss E.V.C. Cooke - Donation	Stipend
Memorial Mrs K. Donald	Sabbath school
R.J. Lyons Bequest	Stipend
Memorial - Ethne Todd	Sabbath school
Memorial - Mary Anne Mc Grew	Sabbath school
Memorial - Mrs D. Orr	P.W.A
Memorial Mrs A. J. Giboney	Sabbath school

Memorials/Donations/Bequests	Purpose
Anonymous	F.W.O
2nd Omagh Donation	Sustentation
Bequest of late James Greer	Sustentation
Bequest of late Hugh Mc Neill	Stipend
Bequest - Wm. B. Mc Neill	Stipend
Late Mr G. B. L. Glasgow	Stipend
Investment - Sale of manse land	Stipend
Anoymous Gift	World Hunger
Anonymous Gift	United Appeal
Memorial - Samuel Sayers	Church Repairs
Bequest of late William Dale	Stipend
Bequest of late Miss Greer	Sabbath school
Memorial - Robt. Fyffe	Church Repairs
Memorial Mrs A. Lewis	Church Repairs
Memorial - Mrs A. J. Giboney	Sabbath school
Anonymous Gift	Sabbath school
Bequest - E. P. Coote	United Appeal
Memorial Miss Mary Mc Farland	Stipend
Memorial - William Somerville	Choir Fund
Memorial - Mrs. A. Roberts	Sustentation
Bequest - Harold Mc Cauley	Church Repairs
Bequest - Miss Jeannie Elliott	Stipend
Memorial - Mrs Isabella Mc Grew	Pres. Orphan Society
Memorial - Mrs Isabella Mc Grew	Mission to Lepers
Bequest of late Matilda Morrow	Committee
Memorial - W. H. Johnson	Church Repairs
Memorial - Norman Mc Clure	Sabbath school
Donation - S & M Reid	Sabbath school
Mrs K.B. Watson - Bequest	Committee
Bequest - Mr & Mrs Jack White	Stipend
Memorial - James C. White	Choir Fund
Bequest Mc Adam Memorial	Stipend
Bequest of late William Hamilton	Sabbath school
Memorial - Mrs Sarah Fyffe	Stipend
Annual Donation-Miss E.Crawfotd	W.F.O.
The Linda,John & Emma Torney	World Development
Memorial Fund	
Bequest - Fred & Blanche Todd	Stipend
Memorial - Ian W.T. Coote	Sabbath school
Memorial - William Arthur	Church Repairs
Mrs E. White	Choir
Robert S. Mc Curdy - Memorial	Sabbath school

The manses

1754-1801 It is not known where Rev Robert Nelson, the first minister, resided.

1803- 1824 Although it is not established for definite, it is probable that Rev David Gilkey lived at Aughnamoyle for much of this period.

1824-1842 Records show that David Gilkey lived at Aughnamoyle in the period 1824 to 1850.
NOTE: Aughnamoyle includes a house accessed from the Derry Road at the Omagh Rugby Club. This house was also occupied by Rev Black, a former Minister of Gillygooley (1842 to 1871), and later by his daughter, Miss Anna Maria Black, who was a prominent member of Trinity congregation and a member of the Church Committee from 1926 to 1932.

1842-1879 Rev Josias Mitchell lived first at Mullaghmore and later (by 1854) at Coneywarren in a house that stood on the site of Rocklow Manse. In Griffiths Valuation of 1860 we see under the townland of Coneywarren that the Rev Josias Mitchell resides there and the owner of the land is Claude Houston. The 'Description of the Tenement' is "House, office and land" covering 22 acres 3 roods 10 perches, with a total rateable value of £25. There is also mention of "House (in progress)". This would confirm that Rocklow was built in 1860. It is worth recording that, when built, Rocklow Manse had no running water, no gas or electric lighting and probably no sewerage system!

New outbuildings at Rocklow Manse - 1863

In June 1863 a specification was drawn up to rebuild the original outhouses that had been left standing. The very detailed specification suggests that the proposed building was the type of barn that is still to be seen on many farms in the country today - a two-storied building with a byre, stables and pig-house on the ground floor and a barn (hay-loft) covering the entire first floor. Foundations were to comprise "large, flat, even-bedded stones". Outside walls were to be 18 inches thick, and inside walls 16 inches thick; mortar was to be "a mixture of clean, sharp sand and well burnt coke lime". Quoins for the corners were to be reclaimed from the old building, and if there was not sufficient of these "the contractor to provide same and these to be hammer dressed". The contractor was also "to take all the old building down and take out all the windows and woodwork as carefully as possible", using "as many stones and bricks from the old building as possible." The roof was to be slated.

The cost of £170 for the rebuilding work seems initially to have been met by Church member John Monteith (retired surgeon). He received back his capital with interest in February 1868.

The next inhabitants of Rocklow Manse were:

1879-1884	Rev Thomas Hamill, MA
1884-1887	Rev William Johnston, BA
1888-1890	Rev James Campbell, BA
1890-1898	Rev Robert Wallace, MA

Rev Wallace lived in the manse at Coneywarren until his death on 24 January 1897. It is thought that Mrs Wallace remained in residence at the manse for some months after her husband's death.

1898-1920   The death of Rev Wallace ended the use of Rocklow as a manse for the next 22 years, for whatever reason.

1898-1927   The Church minutes record that in March 1898 it was:

> proposed by Mr Dale, seconded by Mr Joseph Anderson and passed that the rent for the manse and garden, if let, be fixed at £60 per annum free of taxes. Further, the grazing and meadow and lane attached to the manse be let at £15 for the season.

In April 1898 Rev George Thompson was installed as Minister. While in Omagh he was a bachelor and chose to live at Holmview Terrace, Omagh.

In May 1898 the manse was let to Mrs Eliza Byrne, Rash House, Omagh on a five-year lease at £60 free of taxes.

Dr Thompson's term in Omagh also included a family tragedy. In the week after a major Church extension had been officially opened in October 1901 Dr Thompson's sister, who was visiting for the occasion, became ill and died later at his home. This sad incident may well have influenced his decision to leave Omagh just 18 months later.

On 7 March 1904 it is recorded that the Church Committee asked "Messrs Kirk, Lyons and McConnell to try to let the manse." This time the manse was let to Mrs Murphy from 1 May 1904 at a rent of £50 free of taxes. Eventually, in February 1907, she was given notice to quit on 1 May of that year.

The next Minister, Rev W J Baird, stayed for only one year and did not live in the manse.

Rev R W Morrow lived at Camowen Terrace, Omagh during most of his ministry in the town, which lasted from 1904 to 1926. It should be noted that, in those times, the manse rent went to the Minister. Further, it was his entitlement if he became Senior Minister, even in retirement.

So from 1898 to 1920 Ministers of Second Omagh lived elsewhere in the town. During that time there was considerable debate about the future of Rocklow manse. It seemed to be a drain on Church funds, needing regular repair and maintenance. The Committee, led by

Messrs T C Dickie, Joseph Anderson, Hugh Kirk and John Barr, frequently considered selling it. Purchase of the head rent was also pursued at that time, but the ground landlord was reluctant to agree terms. In 1905 the Greer family purchased land at Coneywarren that included a large house (later to be Coneywarren children's home) and the land on which Rocklow manse was built. Negotiations reopened regarding the sale of the head rent, but eventually an offer of £250 was declined by the Greer estate trustees in August 1907.

In May 1906 an offer of £140 to Dean Galbraith, representing the Methodist Church, for the purchase of a plot of ground convenient to the church was also declined, and once again there was a significant movement within the Committee in favour of selling the manse.

Between the end of Mrs Murphy's tenancy in May 1907 and August 1908 the Church had no success in letting the manse despite several attempts and widespread advertising. Consequently in September 1908 it was "agreed that the Manse and lands be advertised for sale at Public Auction. Before fixing a date, a congregational meeting to be called and have purpose of the sale put before the members." However, on 12 October 1908, before these actions were effected, it was announced that there was "new interest in taking manse on lease." On 16 December 1908 it was finally agreed that Rocklow be let to Major McCormack "after the Committee carry out all improvements suggested by Major McCormack." The rent was £35, plus taxes, for three years. The proposed works included the installation of a new grate in the drawing-room, installing the old grate in a bedroom and providing a "new pan in the closet". The bill for these and other works was £137/12/8.

In June 1919 the Church Committee decided that Major McCormack should be served with a notice to quit. This action was confirmed on 27 October 1919. Following Major McCormack's departure it was agreed on 8 December 1919 that a "preliminary notice of Sale of Rocklow be published in the Tyrone Constitution and the Belfast Evening Telegraph." This action was apparently not pursued, as in August 1920 the Church once again incurred considerable expenditure in repairing the manse. The repairs cost £491/18/0, and the house was insured for £2,000. There followed a call for subscriptions to defray the expenses, and at their monthly meeting the Committee members promised £140. It is believed that the Morrow family lived at the manse from 1920 to 1926.

Rocklow Manse

On 9 February 1927 Rev J H R Gibson was installed as Minister, and he became the first Minister in 29 years to occupy Rocklow for his entire ministry in Omagh. After Rev Gibson's installation and occupancy of the manse, Dr Morrow, as Senior Minister, was still entitled to receive a 'rent'. The congregation addressed the matter by introducing a special "envelope collection" for this purpose on 1 May each year. An interesting footnote to this period is that in 1934 Dr Morrow wrote to surrender any such claim.

The manse continued to incur high maintenance and modernisation costs. In 1941 it was determined that the well water supply in the grounds was not satisfactory. The quality of the water had been a source of continual concern, requiring much attention through the years. In October 1952 prices were obtained for connection to mains water. However, on receipt of the estimate the scheme was further postponed. It was later, in 1953, that mains water was eventually provided. At the same time a tank was installed in the attic and new fittings provided for the bathroom and hot-press.

Sale of Rocklow manse - 1970

The decision to sell Rocklow manse was taken in 1970, following Rev Pinkerton's ministry and before the arrival of Rev RWW Clarke. The old building was in need of much renovation. In particular, the roof timbers were rotting and needed total replacement. A new manse was therefore planned and built on the adjoining site at Coneywarren. The convenor of the manse sub-committee was John Wallace.

In 1971 Rocklow Manse and some adjoining land was sold to Samuel King for £10,000. The new manse was a more modern home with smaller rooms and more efficient heating systems. The first occupant of the new manse was Rev RWW Clarke in 1973. In 2002 the remaining land around the manse was sold to a developer with the intention of updating and relocating the present manse.

This new manse was completed in 1973. The first occupants were the Clarke family.

A group of Elders and Clergy visit the new manse at Coneywarren.
L to R: JA Cathcart, J Crawford, I Stevenson, Rev RH Pinkerton, WH Johnston, Dr JHR Gibson, TJ Robinson, Rev RWW Clarke, H McCauley, D MacKenzie, JC White, H Todd and N McClure.

Church committee members at the new manse. L to R: Rev RWW Clarke, Dr S Gilmour, Dr JM Johnston, W Hamilton, RA Elliott, J Kincaid, Arthur McFarland, F Todd, A Thompson, R McDermott, A McKeeman, G Mullin, R Orr, J Wallace and W Porter.

Wives of committee members at the new manse. L TO R: Mrs J Wallace, Mrs R Elliott, Mrs A McKeeman, Mrs A Thompson, Mrs D Black, Mrs J Kincaid, Mrs G Mullin, Mrs R Johnston, Mrs R Orr, Mrs R McDermott, Mrs S Gilmour, Mrs W Hamilton, Mrs F Todd, Mrs W Porter, Mrs RWW Clarke, Miss Nora McAdam and Mrs Arthur McFarland.

The Girls' Brigade

Contributed by Mavis Jardine

The Girls' Brigade comprises local companies, each of which is connected with a Church or Mission of an approved Christian denomination, and every member attends Church, Bible Class or Sunday School. The Brigade provides activities designed to help girls to attain physical, mental and spiritual maturity and encourages them to express what they learn, through practical service to home, community and Church.

The Brigade was formed in 1965 by the union of:

The Girls' Brigade (Ireland)
Formed in Dublin in 1893 and founded on twin pillars, Bible class and physical training, having as its aim "The extension of Christ's Kingdom amongst girls".

The Girls' Guildry (Scotland)
Founded in 1900 as a Church-centred organisation, providing programmes for four age groups. Its varied activities aimed to help girls to become mature Christian women. An inter-denominational and international movement with a strong emphasis on service to others.

The Girls' Life Brigade (England)
Founded in 1902 by the National Sunday School Union. The aim being "To help and encourage girls to become responsible, self-reliant, useful Christian women".

The Girls' Brigade badge

The sole emblem of the Girls' Brigade is the Girls' Brigade Badge, the design and colour of which may not be altered. It is to be used exclusively by the Brigade.

In the centre is a Cross, the symbol of Christ and his Church. Below the Cross is a lamp, that our light may shine out upon the world; above it, a crown, that we may own Christ as our King; behind all, a torch, the flame of Christ's living Spirit and our devotion to him.

Aims, Principles and Motto

The aim of the Girls' Brigade, being a Christian organisation, international and interdenominational, is: "To help girls become followers of the Lord Jesus Christ, and, through self-control, reverence and a sense of responsibility, to find true enrichment of life". The Brigade acknowledges Jesus Christ as Saviour and Lord according to the Scriptures and seeks to fulfil its aim to the Glory of One God, Father, Son and Holy Spirit. The Brigade witnesses to the standard set by Jesus Christ for the whole of life, and gives positive teaching on the Christian attitude to the social evils facing its members. Its motto is *"Seek, serve and follow Christ"*.

Trinity Girls' Brigade

The name of the Trinity Girls' Brigade first appeared in the annual report of 1960-61. Trinity was enrolled as the 88th Company at the Brigade Council meeting in Dublin in 1960. Miss B Nesbitt of Johnston Park, Omagh became the first Captain and Rev Harry Pinkerton the Chaplain, with an intake of 64 girls.

Miss Nesbitt was Captain until 1964, when Miss Sonia Ewing of Festival Park, Omagh took over, with a total of 85 girls and three officers, including the Minister. Miss Ewing resigned in 1968, and the company was then renumbered as 154th Trinity Omagh Girls' Brigade, losing the 88th moniker because more companies were being formed in Ireland at the time.

From 1968 to 1972, 154th Trinity Girls' Brigade closed down. Then in 1972 Miss Linda Maguire from Johnston Park, Omagh became Captain, a post she held for two years. Mrs B Cox of Sunnycrest Gardens, Omagh took over from 1974 to 1976. Mrs Joyce Smyth from Dergmoney Heights succeeded Mrs Cox, remaining as Captain until 1988. Mrs Mavis Jardine of Gillygooley, Omagh was chosen to follow in Joyce's footsteps, and is still Captain.

New Captain Joyce Smyth making a presentation to outgoing Captain, Mrs Beryl Cox. (1976)

The 154th Trinity company belongs to the West Ulster district, which meets three times a year - September, March and May - when the various events, such as UniHOC, netball and the annual parade, are organised for the incoming session.

Nineteen hundred and ninety-three was the centenary year of the Girls' Brigade, and 154th Trinity attended a Church service and parade in Belfast on 13 June, when all Northern Ireland Brigades were represented. Trinity girls also participated in a centenary display in the Ardhowen Theatre, Enniskillen, along with other Brigades of the West Ulster division.

Over the years, changes have been made to the uniforms. New ceremonial uniforms came into vogue in March 2000, when the company section blazer was exchanged for a navy, V-neck sweater and open-neck white blouse.

There are several sections in the Girls' Brigade, and the programmes and activities vary accordingly. These, together with various awards, are summarised below:

Explorers (5-8 years)

The Explorer programme is divided into six parts: God's Book, Talents and Tasks, Exploring, Activity, Self and Riches. Satisfactory completion of work in the first, second and third years is recognised with copper, silver and gold stars respectively.

Juniors (9-11 years) and Seniors (12-14 years)

These programmes are divided into four subjects over three years: Spiritual, Physical, Educational and Service. The girls are awarded junior and senior circles at the end of each year.

Brigaders (15-20 years)

The Brigaders have to achieve 40 points to gain their Brigader brooch, over a three to four-year period. The programme is divided into the same four subjects as for the junior and senior programmes.

Alison Donnell being presented with her brigader brooch by her mother Pearl

GB Company 1994

Back Row (l to r): Caroline Scott, Amanda Humphrey, Alison McNally, Louise Scott, Julie Martin, Andrea Scott, Morna Jardine, Diane Scott, Lynette Porter.

3rd row: Sub Officer Nicola Campbell, Hazel Armstrong, Jayne Armstrong, Emma-Jayne Simpson, Julie Campbell, Catherine Herron, Leanne Copley, Louise Anthony, Kim Bell, Sub Officer Alison Donnell.

2nd row includes Adele Martin, Mrs Sheena Herron, Rev R Herron (Inspecting Officer), Mrs Mavis Jardine (Captain), Mrs Pearl Donnell (Lieutenant), Mrs Dorothy Simpson (Lieutenant), Holly McQuale, Jolene Bell.

Front row: Emma Carey, Kara Evans, Jolene Bell, Julie Ford, Ashley Allen, Sarah Ferguson, Nicola Scott, Valerie Scott, Judith McGurk, Erin McWilliams.

GB Group with Scripture Shield

Standing (L to R): Adele Hammond, Karen Smyth, Dawn Blayney, Vanda Stewart, Julie Forbes, Elizabeth Johnston and Elaine O'Donnell.

Seated: Rhonda Fleming, Zara Baxter and Captain Helen Ewing.

Colour party May 1975
Back Row (L to R): A Brunt, Joan Finlay, Audrey Finlay, Yvonne Ewing, Mandy Cox, Pamela Ewing.
Front: Lieutenant Linda McGeagh and Captain Beryl Cox.

Platform party 1974
The platform party at the GB annual parents evening 1974
Back row (L to R): Rev J Murdoch, Mrs RWW Clarke, Mrs J MacKenzie, Rev RWW Clarke
Front: Helen Ewing, Linda McGeagh, Mrs Beryl Cox, Mrs Irene Kearns and Mrs Joy Irvine.

The Boys' Brigade

1st Omagh Company Boys' Brigade

The Boys' Brigade movement was founded on 28 February 1883. The first company in Ireland was started by Mr William McVicker in 1888. It is believed that 1st Omagh Company, when it was founded in 1892, was the second in Ireland and the first youth organisation in Omagh. The first Captain was Joseph Anderson, JP (the founder of J B Anderson and Co). At that time the Company had the support of all the Protestant Churches in Omagh, and this remained the case until the Church Lads' Brigade (CLB) movement reached the town in the early twentieth century. The CLB was centred on the Church of Ireland, and quite a number of the original BB members defected, causing a temporary folding of the BB.

The 1st Company was revived in 1905 under the leadership of Rev H W Morrow, the then Minister of Second Omagh (Trinity). Mr T C Dickie, an Elder in the Church, became its President. The Company had the support of both Presbyterian Churches in the town, and this continues to be the case today. The drill hall was the gymnasium of the Royal Inniskilling Fusiliers depot, and the Company met on alternate Fridays, at Second Omagh and First Omagh lecture halls. A Cadet Company was formed for boys between 9 and 12 years. To distinguish them, the Cadets had red braid round their caps, and elastic belts.

In 1908 the members included Sergeants Ernest Orr, Samuel McConnell and James Nelson; Corporals Jack Quigley and James Colhoun; and Lance-Corporals David Clements, Alex McAdam, W J McFarlane and Alfred Armstrong. Annual prizes were awarded to a few boys for "behaviour most exemplary, attendance most regular, progress at drill most marked and general conduct most in keeping with the object and rules of the BB". In addition, there were annual Church parades, football competitions, concerts, charity work at hospitals, the BB Bible classes, and usually an annual excursion or sometimes a camp to Baronscourt, Donaghadee or Portrush, made possible by the kindness of generous friends and inevitably by the ladies of the congregations. Around 30 boys from Omagh attended each of these camps.

In 1911-12 a pipe band was formed. This was an initiative by a Captain Cruikshank, who presented a set of pipes for practice purposes. A jumble sale in the Courthouse raised more funds, with which seven more sets of pipes, two side drums and a bass drum were purchased. Mr J Carson from Edenderry acted as bandmaster, and the Company went on to considerable success and recognition.

War came in 1914, and many former BB members enlisted. A report on the first 20 years of the Brigade states:

"The Omagh Company of the Boys' Brigade has every reason to be proud of the noble and heroic part their former members have taken in the Great War. Those of us who are left behind must never forget, as we can never measure, our debt to the boys who have died that we might live. If our lads had not been more valiant, if they had not been ready to 'lay the world away' the moment the call came, and to go to their death as a routine duty of the day, there would have been an end to all that the members of the Boys' Brigade holds most worthy to be cherished. If today we hold our heads high, with a new pride in our organisation, to whom do we owe it but to those who themselves lie so low? And if that pride is not to be a vain thing it will inspire the desire and the will to be worthy of the immortal memory on which it is founded. We owe to the dead the duty not to hold lightly the heritage which they have won for us. And we have another duty, which is to honour and keep bright that memory. Every family that has given of its manhood to the country's cause is entitled to its own Certificate of Honour - some title-deed of national gratitude which will record how father, son or brother laid down his life at the call."

Captain Cruikshank, who had presented the practice pipes to the Company in 1911, was one of those who made the supreme sacrifice.

Roll of Honour

The following were killed in action,
or died in the service of their Country.

Capt. P. Cruickshank
2nd Lieut. T. L. Clements
2nd Lieut. Jack Wilson
Charles Clements, E.R.A.
Sgt.-Major R. Campbell
Corpl. W. Holland
Private Jack M'Adam
Private W. Nixon
Private Robert Watson

"Their name liveth for evermore".

By 1918-19 the Company strength had risen to 98, which gave Omagh the distinction of being the largest Company in Ireland at that time. It had a very talented gymnastics class, under the instruction of Mr J Dorman. There was also a young ladies' gymnastics class, started in connection with the Company. Together the classes gave quite a few local displays and exhibitions of their talents, the most notable being the Variety Entertainment and Allied Tableaux given in the Town Hall on Monday 16 December 1918.

Despite the arrival of the Boy Scout movement in Omagh in 1919, the BB Company continued to prosper, but its strength ebbed towards the late '20s and it once again ceased to meet.

However, it is recorded in the Church minutes that on 20 March 1930 Mr T J McAdam proposed and Mr R D Swan seconded the following motion:

"That the Church Committee sanction the formation of a company of the Boys' Brigade.

That the Captain should be Captain W H Fyffe MBE; the Lieutenants Albert E Duncan, William Boyd and R S Monteith; and the Instructor Samuel Maguire."

The regenerated Company prided itself on its drill and gymnastics excellence, with the 'wooden horse' being ever-present in the Church hall. The Company pipe band was re-formed, and its music was a feature of that period.

In the 1960s and 1970s the Company had a first-class table tennis squad that regularly excelled in national championships.

1st Omagh BB Company 2004

Chaplains: Rev Robert Herron, Rev John Murdoch
Company Captain: Drew Hamilton
Lieutenants: Mrs Valerie Alexander, Mr Noel Barton.
Warrant Officers: Mrs Isobel Bell, Ms Dorothy Henry, Mrs Mandy Milligan, Mr Alan Duff, Mr David Marshall
Anchor Boys: Justin Aiken, Mark Clements, Matthew Donaldson, Ben Hall, Jack Hill, Deane Kane, Reece Kane, James Kerr, John Kerr, Scott McAleer, Andrew Monteith, James Rutledge, Simon Thompson, Stuart Thompson, Steve Wright.
Junior Section: Jonathan Agnew, Matthew Alexander, Victor Barton, William Barton, Craig Breen, Gary Donaldson, Marcus Donaldson, Darryl Gilchrist, Corporal Simon Graham, Stuart Graham, William Hamilton, Jaymie Hill, Ethan Kane, Lloyd Kane, David Long, Lance Corporal Stephen McConnell, Stuart McFarland, Matthew McKernan, James Marshall, Lee Nesbitt, Clive Sproule, Jason Sproule, Jack Swann, Luke Taylor, Duncan Wright, Mathew Taylor, Mark Wright,
Company Section: Richard Barton, Richard Bell, Richard Clements, David Crawford, Ashley Graham, Daryl Graham, Lance Corporal John Graham, Corporal Simon Graham, Lance Corporal Adam Henry, Staff Sergeant Iain Herron, Malcolm Herron, Matthew Lee, Adam Leitch, Corporal Stephen McConnell, James Marshall, Lance Corporal Andrew Young,

First Company, Boys Brigade at First Omagh Church 1913

1st Omagh Boys' Brigade Pipe Band led the Children's Day Parade in 1937. This is the band in the early 1930s.
Back row: Jim Carson, Tommy Woods, Dick Wilton, D. (Dutchie) Speers, Jay Pollock, Fred Farren, Willie Johnston.
Front row: James Cathcart, Vivian McFarland, Ernie McMichael, Albert McCutcheon, Sam Hall, William Greer,
Jim McGrew.

Members of the First Omagh Junior BB who won the West Ulster Battalion PE competition held in Enniskillen. They are (from left), back row: Fraser Cathcart, Harold Kerr, Rakesh Tandon, Colin Wilson, Malcolm Cathcart. Front row: Anil Tandon, Brian McKibbin and Charles Beattie.

Ronnie Todd, Carl Logan, Davy Scott and Harold Monteith

"BB Camp at Harlech, Wales. August 1983.
L to R: Colin Edwards, Johnny Moore, David Moore, Craig Logan, Mark Brady, Jeremy Brady, Alan Edwards and Alan Moore."

Presentations to departing officers Joe Crozier (left) and Jim Lynch (right) by Mervyn Beattie and John Stewart 1967

The Cruikshank Cup being presented by S Gallagher to S McConnell at centenary celebration 1993

Former BB Captains at Centenary celebrations 1993.
Archie Thomson, Drew Hamilton, John Gordon, Sammy McConnell and Jim Lynch.

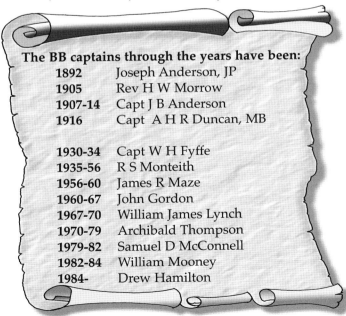

The BB captains through the years have been:

1892	Joseph Anderson, JP
1905	Rev H W Morrow
1907-14	Capt J B Anderson
1916	Capt A H R Duncan, MB
1930-34	Capt W H Fyffe
1935-56	R S Monteith
1956-60	James R Maze
1960-67	John Gordon
1967-70	William James Lynch
1970-79	Archibald Thompson
1979-82	Samuel D McConnell
1982-84	William Mooney
1984-	Drew Hamilton

The Sunday School

Sunday School (or Sabbath School) is an important part of Presbyterianism. Through it the children of the Church learn a Catechism, the Ten Commandments and stories and teachings from the Bible.

Professor John M Barkley, in his 1959 publication 'A Short History of the Presbyterian Church in Ireland', states:

> At the beginning of the nineteenth century there were very few Sunday Schools in Ireland. When the Sunday School Society for Ireland, a non-sectarian body, was founded in 1809, there were but 80 in the whole of Ireland. In 1862 the Sabbath School Society was founded in connection with the Presbyterian Church.

Statistics show that there were approximately 1,000 Sunday Schools in the Presbyterian faith throughout Ireland in the year 1840. This number increased steadily until after 1910, when the figure gradually declined each year. At present there are about 550 Sunday Schools in the whole of Ireland. It is not known when Second Omagh's Sunday School started. The first Church records that can be found date from 1856. We know that until around 1950 there were two Sabbath Schools every Sunday - one in the morning before the Sunday service, and the other in the afternoon or evening. It was normal to have two Superintendents, but the one for the morning School was usually regarded as the senior person. In addition to the Sabbath School, older children attended the Bible Class. These were usually those who were coming of an age where they could understand and become full communicants (full members) of the Church.

It is known that Mr T C Dickie was the Sunday School Superintendent for at least 30 years. This confirms that Second Omagh Sunday School dates back to at least 1878. Details of the early period are scant, but some impressions can be derived from later reports and records. For example, it is recorded that in February 1884 the Sunday School held a 'Soiree' in the Grand Jury rooms of the Court-house, Omagh. This would have been a fund-raising initiative, and the ladies of the Church and Sunday School Teachers all played their part. Helping with catering and organisation on this occasion were: Mrs Dickie, Mrs Kirk, Mrs Hamill, Miss Houston (Mountjoy), Mrs Buchanan (Killyclogher), Mrs Harrison, Mrs McKnight, Mrs George White (Moorlough), Miss Henry, Miss White (Beagh), Mrs White (Market Street.) and Mrs Smyth(Gillygooley); also the Misses McConnell, McAdam, Hall and Allister.

The Sunday School teachers were William Scott, W H Wilson, Mr McAdam, Mrs Hamill (Minister's wife), Miss Hall, Mrs Harrison, Miss McConnell and A J Ferguson. The Superintendent of the Evening Sabbath School was Mr William Dale. Before 1884 it had been Mr Anderson. There were 97 scholars on the Sunday School roll, and the average attendance was 57.

On 5 August 1887 the Tyrone Constitution reported as follows:

> The annual excursion and picnic in connection with Second Omagh Presbyterian Church Sabbath School took place on Monday under most favourable circumstances. At ten o'clock the children, numbering upwards of 200, together with a number of relatives and friends, assembled at the church, and soon after left on well appointed vehicles in charge of their pastor Rev W Johnston, assisted by Rev W Colquhoun, (First Omagh), for Baronscourt, where they were joined by Rev J McFadden, Badoney and Rev A White, Gortin. The proceedings of the day were commenced by the entire party partaking of a substantial lunch after which games of various kinds were engaged in. Towards evening the party assembled in a group and were photographed by Mr JJ Thompson of Omagh.

In 1895-96, pupils on the Superintendent's roll book were: Miss McAdam, Willie Fallows, Jean Wallace, Tom Allen, William Allen, Charlotte Lecky, William Hamilton, Fred Scott, Lena Wallace, George Chisholm, Robert Chisholm, Andrew Graham, Alexander Graham, David McCutcheon, David Graham, Annie Hamilton, Maxwell Chisholm, Deborah Dale, Frank McGrew, Mary A McGrew, Mary A Scott and Susan Lecky.

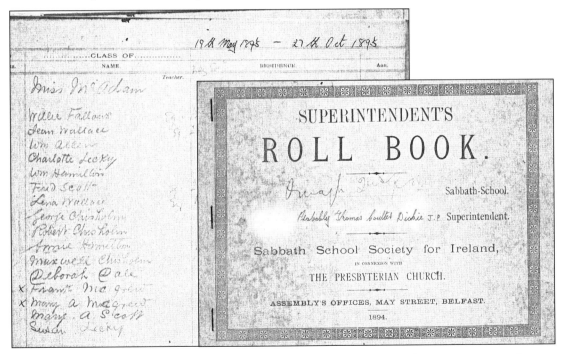

On 30 February 1908 Mr R D Swan was elected to succeed the late T C Dickie as Superintendent of the Sabbath School. That Mr Swan was much loved and respected is reflected in the plaque to his memory located on the wall in the left transept of the Church. In 1928 he was presented with a silver salver in appreciation of his services to the Sunday School.

Further insights into Sunday School life have been provided by a former member.

Interview with Mrs Anne McKane (nee Fenton), who was a Sunday School Teacher in Trinity from about 1930 until December 1942:

> I came from Beragh to live with my aunt, Mrs Donnelly of 16 Campsie Road, Omagh, after her husband died. This was about 1925-1926. I was 10 years old at the time. I joined the Sunday School at Trinity and later the Bible Class, which was taught by the Minister, Mr Gibson. I went straight from Bible Class to teaching in Sunday School. There were two small classes at that time, and towards the end of my time in Trinity (1942) I taught with Mrs Giboney.
>
> I taught the Catechism and verses from the Bible. The children had to behave and know their lessons. I remember teaching Mr Bill McGrew. We had Christmas parties for the children and an excursion in the early summer. We went to places where there was a train service from Omagh: Newcastle, Portrush, Bundoran.When we went to Portrush we had to change trains at Londonderry, walking across the bridge from the City side to the Waterside to get the Portrush train. It was quite a walk for the small children.
>
> We always gave a penny as our Sunday School collection. This money went towards helping a girl in an orphanage in India. At Christmas we would send out small gifts to the other children in the orphanage as well, and we would get a letter back thanking us.

NOTE: *In 1928 Anne Fenton (aged 13) was attending Omagh Model School when she won a Bible and certificate from the Presbyterian Church in Ireland for "repeating the Shorter Catechism from beginning to end, without a mistake, and without any assistance whatsoever."*

On his death in 1932, R D Swan was succeeded as Sunday School Superintendent by R S (Bertie) Monteith, who remained in that post for the next 35 years. This period overlaps comprehensively with the ministry of Rev Harold Pinkerton (1943-1970). Mr Pinkerton had a great love of children. This manifested itself in many ways, but perhaps the abiding memory of most children and adults from that time would be his sermons to the children about the exploits of 'Wee Johnny'.

Wee Johnny

Each Sunday the children and their parents looked forward to hearing what Wee Johnny had been up to in the past week, and they were never disappointed. Wee Johnny's thoughts and deeds, as told by Mr Pinkerton, were light-hearted but always carried a fundamental moral or spiritual message. Below is just one example taken from the book 'Wee Johnny - Stories for Children' by Harry Pinkerton and printed with the kind permission of Mrs M Pinkerton.

Family Heirloom

In Wee Johnny's house there was a very beautiful glass ornament. It had been handed down from generation to generation. Johnny's Mammy was very proud of it. Often she told people the story behind it, how it had belonged to her great-grandmother and how carefully it had been passed on, first to her grandmother, then her mother and then to her. As long as Wee Johnny could remember it had stood in the centre of the drawing room mantelpiece. One day when he had the house to himself he went into the drawing room and stood looking at the ornament. He wondered for a long time if he dare touch it. Then he pulled over a chair and climbed up and reached out his hand. With a firm grip he caught the ornament and was just about to climb down when the chair slipped, Johnny slipped and the ornament slipped and broke into a hundred pieces.

Poor Johnny! He was very silent all evening and no one knew his secret until bedtime. When he was settled in bed he said to his Mammy, "You know that precious ornament, the one that was handed down from generation to generation?" "Yes", says his Mammy, what about it?" "Well", said Johnny, "this generation has dropped it".

You know boys and girls many beautiful things have been handed down to us from generation to generation. We must be careful to hold on to them firmly and not let them drop. Things like the Bible, Sunday, the Church and the Christian faith itself. Many of these things were brought to us by men who gave their lives for them. We must learn to value and respect them. May we never have to make the sad confession Johnny had to make - this generation has dropped it.
(Heritage: Titus ch. 1 v. 9; 2 Timothy ch. 1 vs. 13, 14)

In 1956 when the hall extension was taking place Rev Pinkerton's 'Wee Johnny Club' members were especially active in fund-raising for this project. Each member had a membership card and was enlisted in the effort. The 'thrupenny bit club' raised enough to pay for seats in the new Upper Room, which since that time has been known as the 'Wee Johnny Room'. The new extension was officially opened in 1957.

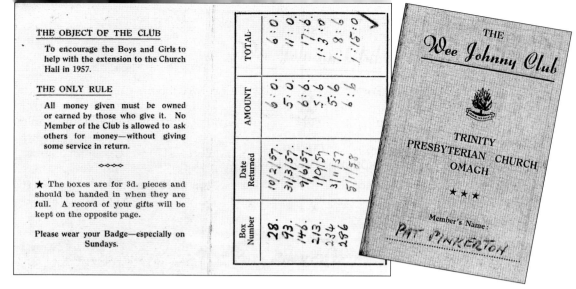

Mr Pinkerton's sense of humour was further illustrated when one Sunday he ended his children's address with the following question: "Children, did you know that we have a boy who has been at Sunday School for more than 50 years?" He went on to explain that he was referring to the Superintendent, Mr R S Monteith, who had progressed from Sunday School to Bible Class to Sunday School Teacher and Superintendent without any break in service. As a token of the congregation's appreciation, Mr Monteith was presented with gold cuff-links by Rev Pinkerton.

Children watching a cine-film in the Church hall. The projectionist, Mr Jack McMillan is seen standing with Rev Pinkerton. Also included are Mrs Giboney (near the projectionist-left), Arthur McFarland, Mrs Pinkerton and Anne Maguire. Note also the old balcony in the hall with a clock. The stairs are at the back (right) and the porch at the hall front door are clearly seen.

The Sunday School roll for 1962 was as follows:

Bill McGrew Junior, Denise Porter, Avril McGrew, Brian McKibbon, Charles Beattie, Joy Craig, Roy Edgar, Valerie Woodside, Noel Hall, Derek Hall, Alan Craig, Harold Carson, Shirley Hussey, Mervyn Maguire, Kenneth Gilmour, Vernon Gilmour, Jim Gilmour, Stanley Gilmour, Alan Porter, Malcolm Cathcart, Michael Thompson, Hilary Anderson, Margaret McGurk, Sandra Weir, Heather Fulton, Rosalind Fulton, Robert McGurk, Ian Gaston, Barbara Millar, Brenda Millar, Linda Elliott, Alan Rankin, Barbara McDermott, John Ivers, Stephen Coulter, Rhoda Campbell, Grace Long, Joy McCay, Richard Roberts, Audrey Roberts, Norman Hemphill, David Boyd, Frazer Cathcart, Linda McGrew, Jennifer Dunn, Albert Bell, Samuel Clarke, Alan Davidson, William Armstrong, Valerie Gilmour and Alan Carson.

In 1967 Mr W McGrew Senior's class was as follows: David Canning, Simon Rankin, Norman Alexander, Tom Clarke, Stephen Coulter, Alan Carson, Robert McGurk, Frazer Cathcart, Ross Hussey, Jim Davidson, Stephen Montgomery, William Armstrong and Alister Cooke.

ATTENDANCE OF SCHOLARS IN

No.	Names	Residence	8th Jan A	R	C	B	15th Jan A	R	C	B	22nd Jan A	R	C	B
16/3/58	David Canning	49, Gortmore Gdns.	5	5	5	5	5	5	5	5	5	5	5	5
14/4/58	Simon Rankin	13, Townview Ave.	5	5	5	5	5	5	5	5	5	5	5	5
17/10/58	Norman Alexander	✓ 20, Beattie Park.	5	5	5	5	5	5	5	5	5	5	5	5
29/1/59	Tom Clarke	Mountfield Road.	5	5	5	5	5	5	5	5	5	5	5	5
17/6/58	Stephen Coulter	7A, Woodvale Ave.	5	5	5	5	5	5	5	5	5	5	5	5
16/6/58	Alan Carson	35, Hospital Rd.	5	5	5	5	5	5	5	5	5	5	5	5
28/8/57	Robt McGurk	2, Beattie Park.	5	5	5	5	5	5	5	5	5	5	5	5
9/6/59	Frazer Cathcart	✓ 37, Gortmore Gdns.	5	5	5	5	5	5	5	5	5	5	5	5
25/2/59	Ross Hussey	✓ 4, Festival Park.	5	5	5	5	5	5	5	5	5	5	5	5
13/6/59	Jim Davidson	✓ 6, Campsie Ave.	5	5	5	5	5	5	5	5	5	5	5	5
26/2/58	Stephen Montgomery	12, Queen's Parade.	5	5	5	5	5	5	5	5	5	5	5	5
9/6/58	William Armstrong.	9, Townview Ave.	5	5	5	5	5	5	5	5	5	5	5	5
18/9/58	Alister Cooke	✓ 7, Beattie Park	5	5	5	5	5	5	5	5	5	5	5	5

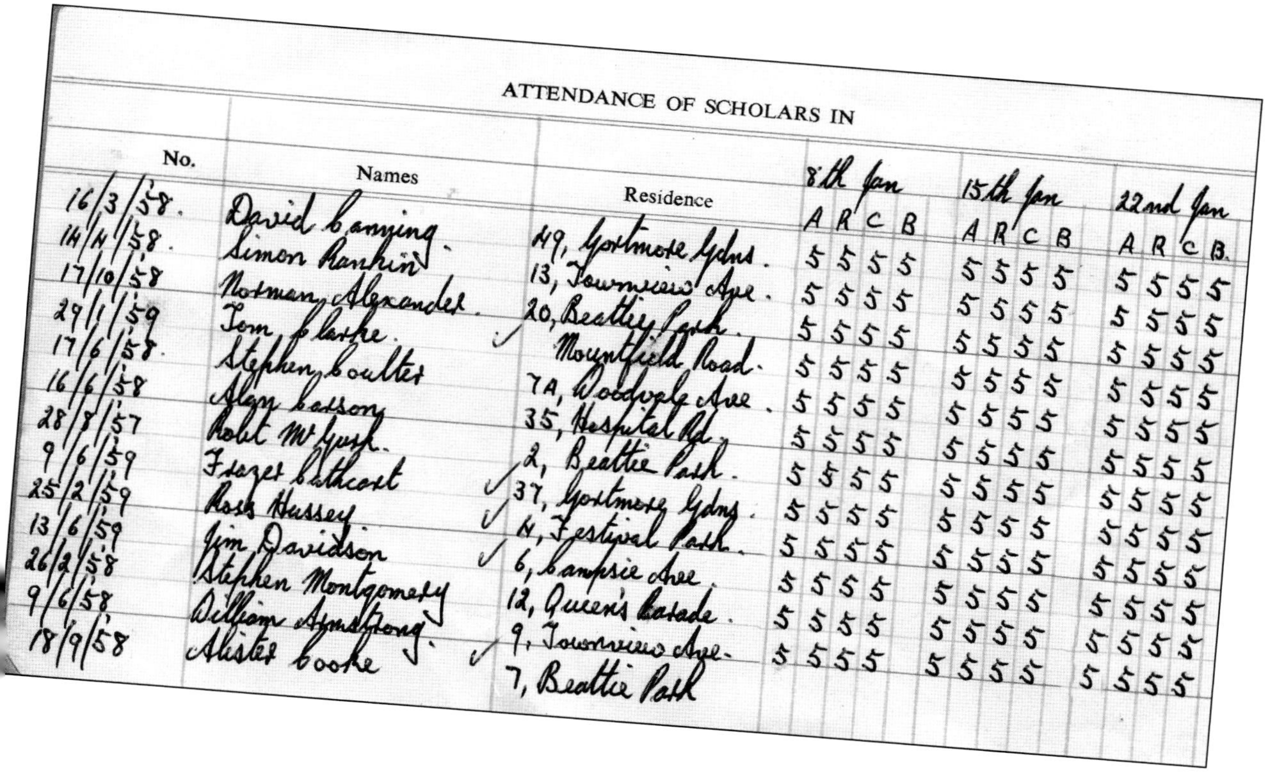

Mrs Annie Jane Giboney 1896-1991

Mrs Giboney was one of the most loved and most highly respected members of Trinity congregation. Her shy and humble nature endeared her to all who knew her. She was a keen member of the indoor bowling club where she was still playing at the age of 85. She loved children and their love for her was reflected in their happy faces as they left for and returned from Sunday School. Every child was known to her and parents had total confidence in their children's safety and well-being when they were with Mrs Giboney.

Annie Livingstone was born in Cavan, Fintona on 16 April 1896. She married William Giboney of Attaghmore, Fintona on 26 June 1919 in Fintona Methodist Church. William was a clerk in Wattersons Coal and Timber Merchants at Scarffe's Entry, Omagh. Initially he and Annie lived at Cavan, Fintona, but, in the early 1930s they moved to Church Street, Omagh and joined Trinity Presbyterian Church where their two sons, Edmund and William, attended the Sunday School and Bible Class. It was around that time that Mrs Giboney became a Sunday School teacher, an experience that she loved, always being involved with the junior pupils. William died on Boxing Day 1952 and in the early 1960s Annie Giboney moved to 36 Johnston Park, Omagh where she lived until a few months before her death on 22 July 1991.

Integration

In March 1976 the integration of Sunday School with morning service was introduced for a trial period. This was a successful experiment and is now the norm. There were 85 boys and girls on the Sunday School roll at that time. Today, there are 78 pupils in the Sunday School and Bible Class.

Trinity Sunday School 1950

Back Row (l to r) includes: Elizabeth Maguire, Roberta Maguire, Betty Nesbitt, Patricia Eaton, Betty Ewart.
Third Row (l to r) includes: Robin Donnell, Ronnie Todd, Douglas Chambers, Roy Todd, Jim Gallagher, Sam Gallagher
Second Row (l to r): Daphne Patterson, Kathleen Moore, Joan Pinkerton, Yvonne McCurdy, Doreen Crawford, Joy Anderson, Valerie Patterson
Front Row (l to r) includes: Phyllis Crawford, Joan McCauley, Anne Todd, Ruth Pinkerton, Jean Gallagher, Carol South and Margaret Coote.

Trinity Sunday School, Easter 1964

Back left: Alan Rankin, Ian Downey, Eric Fyffe, Ian McKibbon, Harold Hussey, Ronnie Hussey, Alan Woodside, Brian McKibbon
Girls (Back Row): Heather Vance, June Parr, Elizabeth Porter, Lorna Coote
Front from left includes: Hilary McDermott, Barbara McDermott, J McGrew, Heather Fulton, Linda Mulholland, Valerie Woodside, Andrea McGrew, Shirley Hussey

Jack, Jean and Robin Wray, who lived on the Kelvin Road

Sunday School 1957

Back Row (l to r): *Brian Burton, Robert Robinson, Keith Vance, Harry Knox, Avril Graham, Ronnie Campbell, Norman Colhoun, Derek Hussey, Ray Gourley, Carole Crowe and Sheena Gilmour.*

Second Row includes: *Jennifer Kinloch, Maud Roberts (teacher), Uel Knox, Lorraine Kinloch, Valerie Anderson, Elizabeth Borland, Mrs Giboney (teacher), Audrey Coote, Dorothy Roberts (teacher), David McGrew, Barbara Rutherdale.*

Third Row includes: *David Cooke, Rosemary Black, Jill McFarland, Harold Hussey, Heather Campbell, Lynda Maguire, Raymond Monteith.*

Front Row includes: *Harold McCay, Keith Gilmour, Audrey Roberts, Robert McGrew, Valerie Graham, Maurice Vance, Heather Vance, Kenny Mullin, Robert Parke, Gregory Parke, Elizabeth Allen, Brian Campbell, Ada Rutherdale and Margaret Rutherdale.*

BB Bible Class c 1950

Back row: Leslie McGrew, Raymond Chesney, Campbell Henderson, Harold Monteith, Albert Johnston, Tom Mansel
Front row: John Mansel, Mr Carson (teacher in Academy) Billy Campbell, Malcolm McClure

Rev Pinkerton watching Santa Claus hand a present to Rosemary Black at the Sunday School party c 1956

Richard Orr (aged 5) presenting a gift to Mrs A Giboney in recognition of thirty years service to the Sunday School. 1972

Sunday School Superintendents

Thomas Coulter Dickie,
Clonavon, Omagh
1878-1908

Robert Douglas Swan,
Ashdene, Omagh
1908-1932

Robert S Monteith,
Dublin Road, Omagh
1932-1967

Andrew Thompson,
Cannondale, Omagh
1967-1982

Neil Gilmour,
Breezemount Park, Omagh
1982-1984

Alice Clarke,
The Manse, Omagh
1985-1990

John McCay,
82, Drumrawn Road,
Drumquin
1991-2004

Adele and Amanda Donald,
31 Slieveard Road, Omagh
2004-

Trinity Bowling Club
- The First Fifty Years

Contributed by Heather Watson.

FIFTY years ago on 14 April 1954, the decision was made to form Trinity Indoor Bowling Club, under the chairmanship of the Rev RH Pinkerton. The following officers were also elected: Secretary, CA Smyth and Treasurer, T Robinson. The club was to be open to all church members over the age of sixteen at the annual subscription of £1.00. Outsiders would be eligible to join but their annual fee was fixed at £1.50. Monday night was to be bowls night and fifty years later this has not changed.

Club rules and bowling card

RULES AND REGULATIONS

1. The Name of the Club shall be "Trinity Indoor Bowling Club, Omagh."

2. The game shall be played in Trinity Church Hall at such times as may be arranged by the Club Committee.

3. The Membership shall consist of Members of Trinity Presbyterian Church, Omagh, and a percentage of Non-Members.

4. The Membership Fee shall be 20/- per annum Single, 30/- Double, or (40/- Family) for those who are Members of the Congregation, and £1 5s. 0d. per annum Single and £2 Double, or (£3 Family) for Non-Members.

   This Fee shall be paid to the Treasurer at the commencement of the Season. Only those over 16 years of age are eligible for Membership

5. All Office-bearers of the Club shall be Members of the Congregation.

RULES—Continued

6. All Membership of the Congregation applying for Membership shall, upon payment of their Membership Fee, automatically become Members. Non-Members of the Congregation desiring to join the Club must be proposed and seconded and approved by the Committee.

7. All Members engaged in the game must wear Bowling or Rubber Shoes (without heels).

8. Unnecessary walking on the "Greens" must be avoided.

9. No unauthorised person to have access to the Club equipment without permission of the Committee.

10. Members wishing to bring a visitor may do so at a Fee of 2/- per night.

11. Play shall not continue after 11 p.m.

Bowlers at their tea break during a match. This was served in the old committee room off the hall balcony. Present from the Trinity team are (l to r)Edgar Weir, Mrs Pinkerton, Rev RH Pinkerton, Mrs South, Mrs Weir, C South, Bobby Vance, JC White.

Quotations were received from Mr J Cathcart and also from Mr D Black for the supply of felt and underfelt. Forth River Bowling Club, Belfast offered the club the loan of bowls during the winter months. The club opened a bank account with the Ulster Bank. The secretary was asked to price bowls from Ms Gamage Ltd and soon the club was ready to begin bowling. The opening night was the 4 October 1954 and Mrs Wilson performed the opening ceremony.

Mr Hamilton, a member of Cookstown club advised Trinity bowlers regarding underfelt and felt. Ash trays and bowling score cards were obtained from Ms Gallagher Ltd.

Edgar Weir throwing a bowl watched by Rev Pinkerton, John Robinson, Charlie South and a visitor.

In 1955, alterations were made to the heating system in the Church Hall by Ms Holmes, Londonderry at a cost of £15/0/0. Mr James White presented two cups to the club for the winners of the 'pairs' competition. Mr John Cathcart also presented two small cups, which were to be the property of the winners. It was decided by the committee members that bowls should be purchased by the club as borrowing bowls was proving to be unsatisfactory.

In 1956 the charge for tea was not thought to be enough and it was fixed at 6d at the AGM on 13 September 1956. Mr James White had provided the ground for Outdoor Bowling at Gortmore Gardens and a fee of £20 per annum was to be paid to him for this. It was also decided to pay £50 to the Church Committee for heating and lighting in the hall.

Great interest being shown during a match at Gortmore Gardens. Among the crowd are Rev Pinkerton and (l to r) Mrs Robinson, Miss Hall, Mrs Millar, Mrs Pollock, Miss Reid, Ann Simpson, Mrs Simpson, Mrs MacKenzie, Mrs Giboney and Miss Elliott.

Photographed in June 1964 (included from left): Wilfie Blackwood, Noelle Blackwood, Dora Manson (nee Graham), Tom Robinson, Lucinda Robinson, Ronnie McDermott, Mrs Roy, Eileen Graham, John Wallace, Tommy Neilly, Rae O'Neill, L Stewart, Bertie Pollock, Ina White, May McFarland, Mabel Johnston, Amy Neilly, Mrs McCappin, Queenie Baillie

Some members of Gortmore Bowling Club.
Back Row (l to r) JC White, Jack Graham, Herbie Moore, Rev RH Pinkerton, Tom Robinson, David Orr, Arthur McFarland, Jim Gourley.
Front Row: Miss Hall, William Martin and Mrs Ina White.

In 1958, £65/19/5 was paid to Mr J C White on account of the pavilion at the outdoor bowling green. When in 1959 the club was growing in members and stature a decision was made to enter the Mid Ulster League as well as running the usual pairs competition. The outdoor bowling was also continuing and £14 was paid to Mr White for repairs to the green.

By 1961 the club was in a very good financial position, £137/9/4 being the credit balance in the bank. Rev Pinkerton gave up the chairmanship of the club and was replaced by Mr Duncan MacKenzie. The Minister of Trinity was to become President of the club. At this time the entry fee for the pairs competition was the pricely sum of 2/=. In 1962 it was decided that outsiders and church members should pay the same subscription to join the club. It was also passed that the 2/= which visitors paid per night should be deleted. New underfelt was purchased from C.A.Anderson at a cost of 18/= per sq.yd. In order to retain interest in the club, two single competitions were to be run with an entrance fee of 1/= per person.

Seventeen years after the formation of the club it boasted a membership of Indoor 51, Outdoor 49. New bowls were also to be purchased at a cost of £6 per pair.

Trinity Indoor Bowling Club 1964
Back Row (l to r): Bobby Vance, Jim
Gourley, Arthur McFarland, Edgar
Weir, Charlie South, W Martin, Jas.
White, J White, Mrs A Orr and
David Orr.
Seated: Mrs Vance, Mrs May
McFarland, Mrs W Martin, Tom
Robinson, Mrs J Pollock, Miss
Reid, Mrs I White, Mrs Millar,
Miss G Orr and Clarke Campbell
On floor: Mrs Pinkerton, G Pollock,
John Pollock, Joan Pinkerton,
Valerie Weir, Pat Pinkerton, C
South and Ruth Pinkerton.

By 1964 the indoor bowling club was still going strong but new top felt had to be purchased as the previous felt had been eaten by mice. By this time a new floor was badly needed in the church hall. After lengthy discussions the Bowling Club Committee decided to make a contribution of £175 towards this. While this work was being done in 1965, Drumragh Club kindly invited the Trinity members to play with them. The pavilion of the outdoor bowling club suffered a burst pipe in mid winter resulting in the carpet and hessian covering being destroyed. New linoleum was to be purchased and varnish for the seats.

In 1970 the membership fees of the club were increased to £1.10.0 but all competitions were to be free. 1971 saw the club winning the most coveted trophy in the Zone, the Moore Cup.

Unfortunately by 1972 the Outdoor Bowling Club was running at a loss. The only solution viable was to increase the membership. Although Trinity had been initially the 1st and indeed only club in the area, by 1973 there were 8 clubs.

By 1974 the committee decided to give an extra £50 to the church for heating & lighting and to also make a contribution of £12.50 towards the cost of a new bell for the church. Club membership was increased to £2 to cover increasing costs.

Rev RWW. & Mrs Clarke presented a marble trophy to the club in 1975. Mr Tom Robinson declined to become Treasurer this year, a position he had held since the formation of the club in 1954, and Mr George Mulholland was elected in his place.

By 1977 the heating in the Church Hall had been improved and the club gave £200 to the Church Committee to help with the costs. The new treasurer Florence Mulholland suggested an increase in membership fees to £2.50 and this was unanimously accepted. Mrs Giboney made a presentation to the club of a trophy, which was to be played for by junior members.

Mrs MacKenzie, whose late husband, Duncan had been a long time member of the club presented the club with a cup in his memory, at the AGM in 1978. This is to be awarded to the person who has the highest score in the weekly rinks.

In 1981 the first national trophy, the National Ladies Four was won by Florence Mullholland, Belle Carmichael, Helen Dunne and Dorothy Orr.

By 1982 it was again deemed necessary to increase the membership fee to £3. By 1986 discussions were taking place between bowling clubs as to the possibility of setting up a new Zone for Mid Tyrone and this happened in the same year. In the next year the annual fee for Trinity Bowling Club was increased to £5 due to the fee to the Zone being increased from £1 per member to £10.

The club continued as usual for the next 10 years, running its annual tournament and entering various competitions with several successes but unfortunately by 1992 the membership had reduced to 10. The club was greatly saddened by the death of some of its long time members and two new trophies were presented in memory of George Mullin and Dorothy Orr.

By the time 1995 arrived there were fears for the life of the club. Many faithful members had been dogged by illness but things turned around and the year was more successful than was anticipated. Once again an increase in membership fees was proposed at the AGM in 1996. It was decided to raise the fee to £10. The death occurred of some members of the club in 2001 and illness forced some others to leave. By this year the membership had dropped to 8 people.

Although the club still continues to function with a low membership it is to be hoped that, in this its fiftieth anniversary year, interest will increase and new members will come and make use of the excellent facilities in Trinity.

The Presbyterian Women's Association

Contributed by Marie Neary

In 1875 the Zenana Missions (the forerunner of the Women's Missionary Association) was formed in Ireland. According to Church House records, Second Omagh joined in 1876 with its contribution of £7/11/4. This began the Church's work with foreign missions. Zenana was an organisation for women, and its aim was to promote Christianity among women of the East.

The Women's Missionary Association (more recently known as the Presbyterian Women's Association) has been a lively, friendly and hard-working force in our Church. Over the years it has supported the Church and its members and has raised much needed funds. Trinity (Second Omagh) Church was at the forefront of women's activity in the province. As a researcher for this book (and occasional visitor at PWA meetings) I have been impressed by the industrious, generous ladies who raised substantial funds for foreign missions, and, later, for home missions by innovative entrepreneurial means. Gallons of tea were drunk - which, as we all know, greatly helps in the process of decision-making!

The PWA/WMA motto is "Go Forward" (from Exodus 14, v 10-31).

Records before 1940 are incomplete, but we do know that Dr Gibson's wife very ably led the WMA before World War II. During the war years Trinity Church hall was requisitioned for war purposes. As there was no hall, Trinity ladies joined First Omagh for WMA meetings, for which they were most grateful. Alternate meetings were held in the Royal Arms Hotel, courtesy of Mrs McIlveen, the hotel housekeeper.

Trinity hall was derequisitioned in October 1944, when Mrs Pinkerton, the new young Minister's wife, presided at the meetings despite the "minor inconvenience" of having a young toddler and twin babies and soon to have another daughter. The other office bearers were Mrs R A Simpson (treasurer) and Mrs Johnston (secretary). Prominent on the Committee were Mrs Matty Monteith and Mrs Jean MacKenzie. Mrs Rutherdale (from Mountjoy East) donated £300 to enable the organisation to start up again.

The bring-and-buy sale (held annually each December for many years) was introduced at that time and brought in necessary funds. Any members having flowers or vegetables to spare brought them to the meetings, and these were sold. Bales of garments were sent to Church House to help destitute people in Europe. Toys and magazines were sent to the General Hospital in Omagh, and members sold things that they had made. All these efforts went to increase funds for the mission boxes.

On the home front, the ladies sent parcels to Trinity members serving with the forces. The local forces and ATS were entertained in the hall, and a canteen was provided on alternate Sunday evenings after the Church service. Mrs Jack White was the first lady to provide tea for members of the Forces, and this example was taken up by quite a few others.

Mrs Mattie Monteith, with her children, Anne and Harold, entertain four soldiers at ther home at Dublin Road, Omagh

Mrs J H Bewglass, the editor of the monthly WMA magazine 'Womens' Work' regularly corresponded with Trinity ladies and paid visits to talk about missionaries in China and India. Each meeting began with a short hymn and prayers, followed by slide or film shows, fellowship and the organisation of fund-raising events. Missionaries on furlough (leave of absence) addressed meetings, further motivating the group. Work parties were organised, where goods were either donated or made up for sale. Lots of knitting and crafts were produced, often using recycled material from old clothes. To help these efforts, wool was sold at a discounted price, from one shilling an ounce, from J B Anderson's shop.

In 1952 Mrs Simpson, the Secretary of Dromore Presbytery (County Down) gave members advice on every field of WMA enterprise. Little had been done for or by women in the foreign mission field before WMA began. At that time the work in China was no longer safe, but the ladies' efforts were still needed in India - for example, in the mission hospital in Borstad. In 1954 the WMA birthday fund was suggested as one way of furthering the work in India by supporting women, who were seeking education as never before. Members of each WMA donated money on their birthday. The birthday fund was originally organised in Trinity Church by Miss McAdam. Mrs McClements took over in 1971.

The 'birth' of the PWA

In February 1971 it was announced that the WMA and the Women's Home Missions were being united to form an organisation to be known as the Presbyterian Women's Association. The bulk of the money raised would go to the general fund, four fifths to Foreign Missions and one fifth to Home Missions. The Women's Home Mission played a useful part in the life of our cities. Deaconesses would visit homes and bring comfort and encouragement to the women. The Home Mission helps the small congregations by giving grants for the upkeep of Churches and the supply of Ministers. There was also a 'Live Wire' scheme, which was run by the children of the Church. The money raised was used to install electricity in the new Churches.

On 12 October 1971 we welcomed Rev and Mrs Clarke to our newly named PWA. Mrs Clarke became the new President and, with her hard work and dedication to duty, was an inspiration to all our members. In time, with Mrs Clarke's encouragement, the ladies of Gillygooley Church joined Trinity PWA. These ladies have made a valuable contribution to the association, both in enthusiasm and in generosity, not to mention their fine baking skills.

In October 1974 Mr McQuillan of the Presbyterian Residential Trust gave an interesting and enlightening talk. The trust exists to provide homes for the elderly. By 1974 it had established four homes - two in Belfast, one in Portrush and one in Newcastle. Rev Clarke expressed the hope that Mr McQuillan's talk would bring further developments in the opening of a Trust house in the Omagh area. So began the foundation for the building of the Harold McCauley home in the town.

In more recent times, during the presidencies of Mrs Clarke, Mrs Parke, Mrs Knox and Mrs Herron, many guest speakers have been drawn from the local community. On one occasion Emma Duffield and Rosemary King spoke on the Ulster Project.

The organisation of Church events was important for fund-raising. In the 1970s and 1980s the twice-yearly jumble sales beat their target figures every year, as did the annual sale of work in December. The PWA annual outing in May was an important and popular event where members really enjoyed the shopping, food and companionship.

Today, times have changed. Most members have careers and family commitments. The pattern of meetings is different, but the topics reflect modern-day values and beliefs.

The Presidents of Trinity WMA/PWA are as follows:

Mrs M Pinkerton	(1944-1950)
Mrs J M Johnston	(1950-1952)
Mrs Bulmer	(1952-1953)
Mrs Pinkerton	(1953-1971)
Mrs A Clarke	(1971-1992)
Mrs O Parke	(1992-1993)
Mrs A Knox	(1993-1994)
Mrs S Herron	(1994-present day)

Ruth Millar
Secretary 1982-84

Agnes Knox
President 1993-94

Six octogenarians (l to r): Mrs Mary Pinkerton, Mrs Madge McKeown (d), Mrs
Florence Cathcart, Mrs Isobel Porter, Mrs Beth Black (d) and Mrs Olive Parke (2002)

Joan Cummins and Dorothy King (2003)

Mrs J M Johnston
President 1950-52

Sheena Herron presents flowers to Mrs Florence Cathcart (2003)

Eileen Coote

Presidents (l to r): Mrs Mary Pinkerton (1944-50 and 1953-71),
Mrs Sheena Herron (1994-present) and Mrs Alice Clarke (1971-92)

Music in Second Omagh/Trinity (1752-2003)

Contributed by RA Elliott

PRIOR to the introduction of musical instruments into Churches, it is understood that, from the 1750s, praise in the Calvanistic Churches was led by a 'precentor', a cleric or lay person who intoned the first note or notes of a very limited number of tunes.

Little is known about the singing in Second Omagh prior to 1856, when the church was rebuilt. It is recorded that George Booth led the Psalmody from around 1850 to 1870. Soon after that Mr T J McAdam took the lead. It is known that, from 1856 until 1901 when the Church was further extended, the choir sat in the gallery and led the praise, without music, from that location. With the introduction of an organ in 1903 the choir moved to the front of the church.

The first pipe organ erected in an Irish Presbyterian Church was that in Newtownbreda, Belfast in 1881. It is recorded that some other 'offending' Churches could only boast of harmoniums. The word 'offending' is used because up to that time there was a serious division as to whether instrumental music should be provided in Churches. Some called it 'the devil's music'! The question was considered by the General Assembly at its meeting in Dublin in 1881 and caused fierce debate and great divisions. Those in favour of musical accompaniment, the 'instrumentalists', provided a special train from Belfast to Dublin and free overnight quarters for those who could be depended upon "to vote straight for the organ". The 'instrumentalists' won the day.

It is known that in Omagh, at a function (not in the Church) in 1884, the choir was accompanied by Mrs Taylor at the harmonium. Also in 1888, at a soiree in the Assembly Hall (at the Court-house) to celebrate the installation of Rev Campbell, Mrs Taylor presided at the organ, which the Tyrone Constitution described as "an exceedingly sweet-toned instrument built on American principle, kindly placed at the disposal of the committee of Second Omagh by Mr J G R Porter", who was the proprietor of the Royal Arms Hotel.

It was to be 1903 before Second Omagh felt able to provide a harmonium in the Church. Even then there was opposition, and only after reflection was it approved. The initiative came from the Church Session, at that time led by T J McAdam, Clerk of Session. He was an accomplished vocalist who was to go on to achieve the amazing record of being a choir member for 80 years. On 28 October 1903, T J McAdam wrote to the Church Committee as follows:

"J.K. McConnell, Esq.
Secretary,
Committee of Second Omagh Presbyterian Church

Dear Sir,

At a meeting of the Session held on 13th October, 1903 the resolution herewith was passed unanimously and a copy ordered to be sent to you as the secretary of committee.

Yours sincerely,
T J McAdam, Clerk of Session."

Proposed by J Anderson, Esq and seconded by TC Dickie, Esq:

That we recommend that a harmonium for the purpose of assisting the praise service be provided and we authorise it to be used in public worship, and as the congregation has already approved almost unanimously of the use of hymns in addition to the Psalms, we recommend copies of the Church Hymnary be procured for Church worship and that a copy of this resolution be laid before Committee at their next meeting. - Passed unanimously.

J.K. McConnell Esq. Secretary Committee
Second Omagh Presbyterian Church.
Dear Sir
At a meeting of the Session of 2nd Omagh P.C
held on Tuesday 13th Octr. 1903 the resolution herewith
was passed unanimously and a copy ordered to be sent
to you as the Secretary of Committee.
Yrs sincerely
T. J. McAdam. Clk of Session
Proposed by J Anderson Esq. Sec'd by T.C. Dickie Esq
That we recommend that a harmonium for the
purpose of assisting the Praise Service be provided,
and we authorise it to be used in public worship,
and as the congregation has already approved almost
unanimously of the use of Hymns in addition to the
Psalms that we recommend copies of the Church
Hymnary to be procured for church worship & that
a copy of this resolution be laid before Committee at
their next meeting - Passed unanimously"

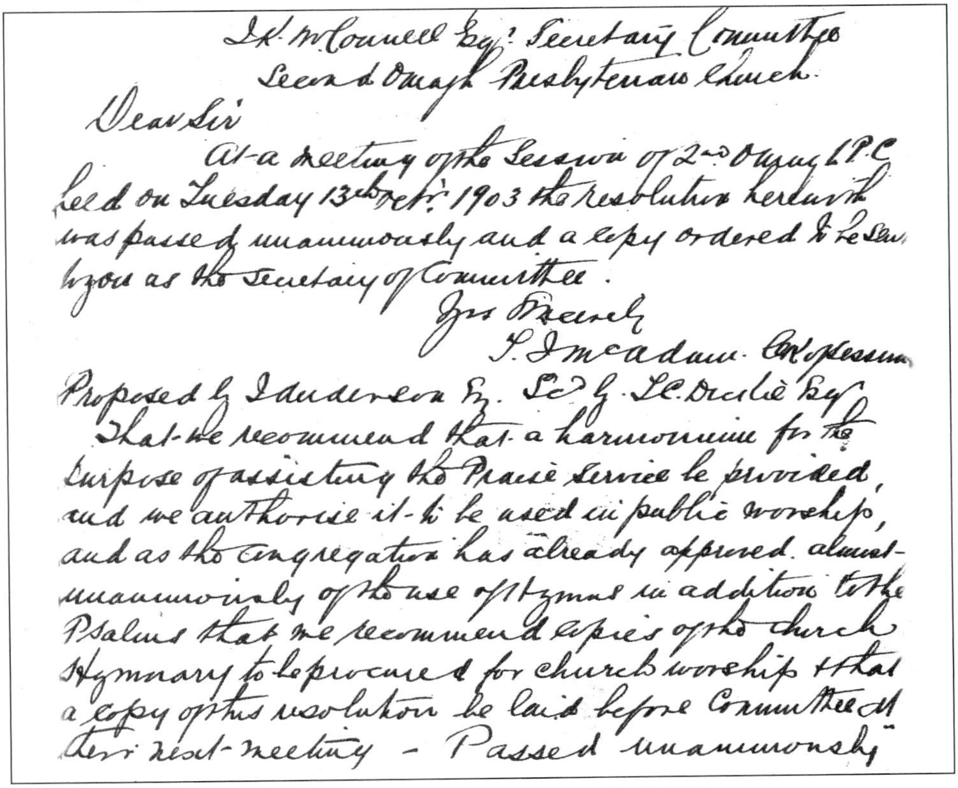

Extract from Trinity Church minutes, Nov 2, 1903

The Church Committee discussed this matter on 2 November 1903, when seven members expressed their opinion in favour of having the harmonium. However, three members opposed the proposal. Consequently it was moved and agreed that the discussion be postponed for the present.

Later, on 7 December 1903, the following motion, proposed and seconded by Messrs Campbell and Kirk, was unanimously agreed:

> That we acquiesce in resolution passed by Session, and that we sanction the raising of necessary funds to provide same by voluntary contributions.

Even then there was not total acceptance of the need to introduce instrumental music into the Church services. This mood is well captured in a satirical poem by an unknown member of the congregation. The rather cheeky hand written verses are on YMCA notepaper. They were clearly written around 1903. The document was forwarded to Rev Herron in May 2001.

SECOND OMAGH HURDY GURDY

Oh dear we have got the organ
And very soon it will be
The beads and cross and cruifix
And Holy Water three.

But still we are not filled
We want an altar too
We must go up to Father Barney
And see what he can do.

And then when she begins to play
Oh dear it is such a drum
It gives us all a headache
And makes the frightened run.

But it is to help poor T.J.
For his thrapple's giving up
But if he had got a salary
It would a lasted long enough.

He don't like to work for nothing
Oh , that could not be.
For he likes to charge two prices
For drugs for you and me.

Then oh it will be to pay for
But we have always got a trick
We shall get a big subscription
From Lord and Lady Kirk

And then Her Majesty McKnight
Will give us somethings, don't you know
She seems to give it with a heart
But it is only for a show.

The organ was proposed before
In Mr Thompson's time
But he said he would not have it
As they weren't of one mind.

But now we have got another man
Who wants to rise a row
Mr Thompson was a gentleman
That's what we have not now

And then we have got some members
They are just next to the roughs,
We have bankrupts, upstarts, pickpockets
And all the gather-ups.

It was Joe proposed the organ
And he would have been a better man
If he had proposed to pay his debts
And let the organ stand.

It was seconded by J.A.C
That man that thinks he's smart
He has got such a flourish
That he would really make you start.

The resolution to have instrumental music in the Church raised many discussions about how the harmonium music would be introduced. Eventually a sub-committee consisting of Mrs Dickie, Mrs Taylor (Organist), Mrs Houston, Mrs Baird (wife of the Minister), Rev Baird, T J McAdam and J K McConnell was appointed to investigate options and implement the recommendation. In January 1904 the four ladies on this committee travelled to Belfast "to select an instrument for use in the Church which they would consider suitable."

It is believed that Mrs Taylor was the first Church organist in Second Omagh from that time, and the absence of further reference to this matter in the Church minutes suggests that the harmonium was well received by the congregation. A practical issue, however, probably prompted the Committee in 1908 to agree "to pay the sexton's son 6d per week for 'blowing the organ on Sundays.'"

This photo shows the pulpit and surround as it was following the renovations of 1901. Note the absence of organ pipes. The present organ and pipes were installed in 1940.

Much later, in November 1928, on the proposal of Mr J K McConnell, seconded by Mr David Black, the Church Committee agreed that a small harmonium be purchased at £10 for use in the Session room. Also at that time, the Committee agreed that "72 copies of the New Psalter and Hymnary at 1/6d be purchased for the Sabbath School, the prayer meeting and the soldiers."

The next recorded Organist after Mrs Taylor is Mrs Moorehead, who played in Trinity from at least 1930 until she left for Belfast in 1934. Mrs Moorehead was paid £10 per year "as a gift" for her services.

After Mrs Moorehead, Miss Eileen Hall and, occasionally, Miss Gertie Hall shared organ duties with the Minister's wife, Mrs Gibson, who later became the regular organist and continued as such until the Gibsons left Trinity in 1942. Interestingly, Miss Hall became Mrs Gallagher and was the mother of our present Clerk of Session, Samuel Gallagher. Eileen Hall also played the piano in Miller's picture house, which later became the Royal Arms ballroom, during the 'silent pictures'.

A visitation to Trinity Church by the Omagh Presbytery in 1936 records that

> they note with great satisfaction, the hearty and acceptable manner in which the musical part of the service is conducted and they rejoice to find that Mr McAdam, who has rendered a long and faithful service in the choir for 72 years, finds delight in still leading the choir in the exalted duty of rendering praise service to God and that he is ably assisted by Mrs Gibson who presides at the organ.

T J McAdam was Choirmaster for more than 50 years, including many years prior to 1903 when the singing was unaccompanied. In all, he was a member of the choir for 80 years, having joined at the age of 9. It is recounted that, in order to ensure that the choir commenced singing at the correct time, he would beat the floor with his foot, counting 'One, two, one, two, three.' It is unlikely that his record years of choir service will ever be beaten.

Plaque at Buchanan organ

It was in 1940 that Trinity received as a gift its wonderful pipe organ, the bequest of the late Lieutenant-Colonel Andrew Buchanan. A brass plaque below the organ pipes bears the following inscription:

> This organ and pulpit, erected to the glory of God, are the gift of the late Lieutenant-Colonel Andrew Buchanan, MA, MD, and his wife, Mary Kyd Buchanan. Colonel Buchanan, formerly of Killyclogher, worshipped in this Church in his youth and afterwards had a distinguished career in the Indian medical service. June 1940

The dedication service was conducted in June 1940 by Rev J McIlrath, BA, Senior Minister of Richview Presbyterian Church, Belfast, who was closely acquainted with Colonel Buchanan in his early days at Queen's University, Belfast and who was a lifelong friend of the late Dr H W Morrow, MA, a former Minister of Trinity Church. Rev McIlrath stated that while at Queen's, Colonel Buchanan had graduated in Arts with First Class Honours and a Gold Medal. They had rooms in Assembly's College, and Colonel Buchanan may have had thoughts of entering the Ministry. However, the Colonel obtained degrees of MD and MCh.

After practical training in a London hospital he joined the Indian medical service in 1884, from which he retired after 28 years' service. Subsequently he practised as a civil surgeon in the Central Provinces of India. He was a pioneer in pathological research and produced medical works of such value that one, at least, on malarial fevers became a textbook for medical students in India. In their later years Colonel Buchanan and his wife lived in Guernsey, but they loved to visit Omagh, and Mrs Buchanan's cultured musical voice was often heard in Trinity.

The pulpit and choir enclosure were made to match the panelling of the organ. The enclosure was subsequently enlarged to accommodate chairs which were presented by Mrs Florence Cathcart in memory of her husband, John, who had been an Elder and Secretary of the Church Committee.

Mrs Gibson

Mrs Gibson was the first organist to play the new instrument. Following its installation, Rev Gibson was approached by several persons regarding the old organ. It was agreed that it should be sold to the best advantage of the Church. With regard to 'the other organ' (perhaps the harmonium that had been purchased for £10), it was felt that "there was no point in keeping it as there was a good piano in the hall already and that First Omagh had asked for the loan of it, so it was decided to let them have it for the duration of the war." There is no record of this "organ" having been returned! On 27 January 1941 "Mr Gibson reported that the old organ had been sold to Badoney Presbyterian Church for £30. This was considered satisfactory and approved."

After Mrs Gibson, Mrs Woods filled the position of Church Organist in a temporary capacity for about two years. In May 1943 four persons were interviewed for the position. Possibly reflecting the quality of the organ and the congregation's pride in it, an expert musician was brought from County Antrim to hear the applicants, but no-one was appointed.

Mrs Simpson, then a member of the choir, was approached. Having agreed to a temporary arrangement, she played the organ for 13 years, although for at least a few years (1945-48), perhaps on a relief basis, a young man, Mr George Campbell, also played. Mrs Simpson always maintained that she helped out "in a temporary and voluntary capacity" and several times asked to be relieved of the responsibility. During her time as Organist many compliments were paid to herself, the choir and their music.

During her tenure several gifts were presented to her by a grateful Church Session. On one occasion she was presented with a new bicycle, on another with an "electric cleaner". When she eventually managed to resign, in February 1956, she was presented with a television set.

From 1956 until 1968 the Organist was the late Jack Anderson. Jack was a banker in Omagh. Unfortunately, he was transferred to Fermanagh and later to Coleraine. He was a wonderful choirmaster and was particularly good with children. When in Omagh he was leader of the Choral Society and arranged concerts with such notable soloists as Owen Brannigan and Brendan O'Dowda. When he left Omagh he continued as an organist in Portstewart, where he died in his nineties. He contributed not only to the music in Trinity but also to the wider Omagh community.

From time to time in the '60s Rev Jack Richardson of Hillhall, then a student, acted as temporary Organist.

From 1969 until 1971 the Organist was Jack Blair, BA, who was the Principal of Castlederg High School. He was an excellent musician and an experienced choirmaster who would not tolerate second-best. Temperamentally, he let the choir know when they were not performing well. He insisted on having an 'introit' at the beginning of each service and was a hard taskmaster at choir practices. However, the choir did perform excellently. Jack was a marvellous exponent of Bach and had the ability to orchestrate a melody at unbelievable speed.

Lorna Baxter

Victor Leitch

Rev. Arthur O'Neill

In an interim period Trinity was assisted by several organists, including Lorna Baxter, and Victor Leitch. At this time also Rev Arthur O'Neill from Fintona acted as choirmaster.

Trinity has been well blessed with excellent Organists over the years, and the present incumbent, Stanley Matthews, is no exception. He first played in the Church as a youth and was appointed Organist in 1972 at 18 years of age. Even then he was a wonderful musician, but he had little experience as a choirmaster. Today he has learned his trade well and is one of the best choirmasters with whom I [R A Elliott] have ever worked. He is respected and well liked by all the choir members, not only for his musicianship but also for his sense of humour. His personal achievements include that of being invited as visiting Organist to St Patrick's Church of Ireland Cathedral in Armagh.

During Stanley's time in charge the choir was robed in 1989, thanks to the benevolence of Blanche and Fred Todd. At that time the choir was so large that some pews had to be used by the younger members. Alas, this is no longer necessary, and recruitment of younger members is increasingly difficult. When Stanley has been unavoidably absent in more recent times we have been very competently helped out by Roy Millar, Sheena Herron and Wendy McCay. In more recent years Wendy Smyth has joined the team as Leader of the Junior Choir. Her talents are reflected in the children's smiling faces and wonderful, happy tuneful singing on Children's Day and at Christmas services.

Sheena Herron   *Wendy McCay*   *Roy Millar*   *Wendy Smyth*

In 1991 the organ required a major overhaul and renovations. The opportunity was taken to enhance its quality by adding a second chamber, thus creating more variety and a richer tone. The services of the eminent organist Stephen Hamill, BSc, LTCL, the Organist at Cooke Centenary Presbyterian Church, Belfast were retained to advise on work specification and generally to be our organ consultant. The cost of the works was some £40,000, and the instrument was officially 'brought back into action' at a recital given by Stephen Hamill.

Photo taken at the rededication of the Buchanan Organ following major renovations and improvements in 1991 (l to r): Rev RWW Clarke, Mr Jack Sloan (Abbey Organ Company), Rev John Shields, Senior Army Chaplain (NI) and Stanley Matthews (Organist and Choirmaster).

Returning to Stanley Matthews, I [R A Elliott] recall that after one Harvest service I was asked to propose a vote of thanks to the ladies who had provided the tea. I did so but took the opportunity to praise Stanley for his work. I said that the other Stanley Matthews had been knighted by the Queen, that we were unable to give our Stanley such an accolade, but could get him a piano to complement the music in Church - something that was dear to his heart. My suggestion was that if members of the congregation so wished they could give contributions to any member of the choir. Next morning a lady telephoned Rev Clarke and undertook to meet the cost of a good piano. That lady was the late Denise White, and the piano was dedicated to the memory of her late parents, Jack and Sarah Louise White.

In past years Trinity has been blessed with some brilliant individual soloists. These have included the legendary T J McAdam, Mattie Monteith, Anne Monteith and Audrey Roberts. This trend continues today where gifted soloists and musicians abound within the congregation.

In addition, the following people are fondly remembered for their singing in the choir:

Ladies	Gentlemen
Greta Carson	Billy Hamilton
Agnes Cathcart	Duncan MacKenzie (former choirmaster)
Eileen Coote	Norman McClure
Jean Coote	Bertie and Harold Monteith
Tillie Grives (nee Torrens)	Herbie Moore
Norah McAdam	George Mullin
Dorothy McKillop	Jim Preston
Eileen Montgomery	Ben Sheehan
Ann Simpson	Jim Sheehan
Violet Torrens	Arthur Simpson
Aileen Walsh	Charlie South
	Andy Thompson

The present choir members are:

Gentlemen: Sammy Gallagher, Noel Donald, Roy Wilkinson, Bob Elliott, Ronnie Hussey and John Moore. (At special times of the year we have the excellent assistance of Joe Gilmour.)

Ladies: Mrs Joan Cummins, Mrs Heather Watson, Mrs Caroline Hussey, Mrs Mavis Jardine, Mrs Marie Neary, Mrs Fran Young, Miss Gladys Cuthbertson, Mrs Dawn Graham, Mrs Beverly Large, Mrs Jeannette Miller, Mrs Claire McElhinney and Mrs Irene Knox.

The World War years

THE Church has seen quite a few wars, including the two world wars of the twentieth century, and its members are included among those who made the supreme sacrifice. During World War I, Omagh was a major garrison town for allied forces. It was from their billets in Omagh that many soldiers began the long journey to the front. Troops attended morning services in their respective churches and Trinity Church organised a special social event for allied forces every Sunday evening in the church hall.

In 1922 a memorial was erected and dedicated to those members of our congregation who lost their lives in World War I.

Marching past Trinity Church, John Street, Omagh on 6th August, 1914.
The 2nd Battalion Royal Inniskilling Fusiliers, including many men from Omagh and District, go off to war. They were to fight at Le Cateau, The Retreat from Mons, the Battle of the Marne, The Aisne, First Ypres and Neuve Chapelle. Very few of the original drafts survived to participate in the Battle of the Somme (July-November 1916). The officer on the horse in the centre ot the picture looking at the camera is Lieutenant (later Major) C.A.M. (Charlie) Alexander of Termon House, Carrickmore, who was trasport officer for the battalion.

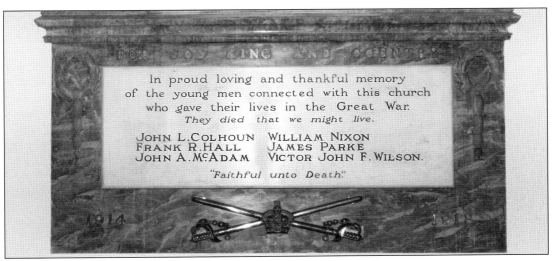

In proud loving and thankful memory
of the young men connected with this church
who gave their lives in the Great War.
They died that we might live.

JOHN L. COLHOUN   WILLIAM NIXON
FRANK R. HALL   JAMES PARKE
JOHN A. McADAM   VICTOR JOHN F. WILSON

"Faithful unto Death."

1914   1918

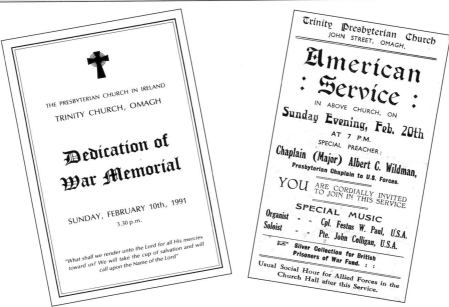

THE PRESBYTERIAN CHURCH IN IRELAND

TRINITY CHURCH, OMAGH

Dedication of War Memorial

SUNDAY, FEBRUARY 10th, 1991

3.30 p.m.

"What shall we render unto the Lord for all His mercies toward us? We will take the cup of salvation and will call upon the Name of the Lord"

Trinity Presbyterian Church
JOHN STREET, OMAGH.

American : Service :

IN ABOVE CHURCH, ON

Sunday Evening, Feb. 20th

AT 7 P.M.

SPECIAL PREACHER:

Chaplain (Major) Albert C. Wildman,
Presbyterian Chaplain to U.S. Forces.

YOU ARE CORDIALLY INVITED TO JOIN IN THIS SERVICE

SPECIAL MUSIC

Organist - - Cpl. Festus W. Paul, U.S.A.
Soloist - - Pte. John Colligan, U.S.A.

☞ Silver Collection for British Prisoners of War Fund. : :

Usual Social Hour for Allied Forces in the Church Hall after this Service.

During the 1939-46 war the congregation of Trinity was entangled in the strife and suffering of the time, in common with most communities throughout Europe. Canteens for feeding the military were established in several locations in Omagh. One such place was Trinity Church hall, which was requisitioned. More detail on this and on how Church members supported the war effort is included in the section on the Women's Missionary Association. The army paraded to Church each Sunday. A parade of soldiers came up Castle Street, 'dropping off' worshippers at each Church - Roman Catholic, Church of Ireland, Methodist and finally Presbyterian. Some seats in the right transept in Trinity were reserved for the armed forces.

Marching down Castle Street; note the gas masks over the shoulders of the soldiers.

It is understood that the Buchanan organ in Trinity (installed 1940) was the last organ in the United Kingdom to be installed until the war ended.

Extracts from Church minutes 1939-1946

The following extracts from the Church minutes of those years reveal some of the war issues that interfaced with Church life and Church property:

2 October 1939 — No action to be taken regarding Church extension during the war. The matter of blacking out of the Church to be left in Mr Cathcart's hands.

24 January 1940 — The best thanks of the Committee and Session be conveyed to Messrs J B Anderson and Co for their generous contribution of material for black-out and to Mr T J Cathcart for his work in connection with same.

19 April 1940 — Military authorities had agreed to pay £11 compensation for damage done to the hall during their occupation, the Committee to take over the black-out at £3. Agreed, on the understanding that the hall would be cleaned before taking over.

7 October 1941 — Agreed that occasional parcels of tobacco and cigarettes be sent to any who were connected with our Church and are at present prisoners of war.

27 January 1942 — Thirty-six forms had been hired to the military. It was proposed that six shillings per week be charged. Agreed.
NOTE: £8/14/0 was duly received on 11 August 1942. "for hire of forms".

8 December 1942 — It was decided to take no action at the moment about trying to get possession of the Church Hall from the military.

11 January 1943 — Letter from the military authorities saying that they were proposing to de-requisition Trinity Hall and offering discussions on any claim for damages that the Church might have.

25 January 1943	Cost of restoring hall to its previous condition was estimated at £80.
April 1943	Military offer of £50 was rejected.
April 1943	It was decided to take down the black-out.
August 1943	It was suggested that the evening services could be held in the hall during the black-out.
14 September 1943	J B Anderson and Co offered to properly 'black-out' the Church at a special price of £28/12/0.
8 October 1943	Military authorities had returned 23 forms, some of which were broken and required repairs. As 33 forms had been supplied, agreed to request that the remaining 10 be returned and that repairs be carried out OR payment of £58 to make up the difference.
28 April 1944	Agreed that the Food Office be granted use of Trinity Hall for the purpose of distributing Ration Books from 22 May till 17 June at 15 shillings per week.
28 June 1944	Reported that a former member of the Church Choir, Corporal Eric Boyd, had been killed in action in Normandy. Agreed that a letter of sympathy be passed to the family.
31 October 1944	Reported that the Church roof needed urgent repairs but, as it would be impossible to get timber at that time, it should be left in the meantime.
29 October 1945	Application from B. Specials for the use of the hall on one evening per week. This was not granted.
	Noted that the supply of coke for the hall heating was very poor quality. Agreed to contact the Coal Controller and ask for an increased ration as the hall was much used by youth organisations.
	Agreed to express the congregation's gratitude to congregation members who had served in the armed forces by presenting each with an inscribed bible.
	Also agreed to have black-outs removed from the Church.
28 January 1946	During the war years the military had been allowed to occupy the centre of the Church. It was agreed that they should now go back to their original seats in the right transept.

Trinity during the 'troubles'

Contributed by Rev RWW Clarke

MY ministry in Omagh coincided comprehensively with that period in Northern Ireland's history known as "The Troubles". We moved to Omagh in April of 1971 and lived for a period of two years in the New Bungalow (as it was called) in the townland of Fireagh, on the Dromore Road. During that period the new Manse (as it was called) was designed, planned and built on its existing site, so I had time to 'get the feel' of the town and where the congregational members lived. As far as I remember, the number of families in Trinity was around 200 - 250 and those in the congregation of Gillygooley numbered 70 plus. During the next 21 years our numbers in Trinity rose to 350 and Gillygooley's numbers kept steady. It was a crowded ministry!

It was a very sad part of my responsibility to share with my clerical brethren in the funerals of the victims of the violence. I think, indeed, that 'The Troubles', instead of dividing the community, helped to strengthen it. Admittedly, like most Ulster towns, Omagh had its own 'no go' areas for both army and police. Nationalism was strong and so was Unionism and it was wise to recognise the threat inherent in such a situation. In the event, there was very little public violence and much increasing good will. Having just come from across the Border, where I ministered in Dundalk for 21 years, and being a native of the Republic (County Monaghan), I was unused to any kind of overt sectarian bitterness. We got on well with one another and our people were proud of their Irish and British identity. It was therefore my great relief to discover that this basically was the position in Omagh, when, with a deal of misgiving, we went to live there. There was a wonderful community spirit, people related well to one another (as they do still) and one was forced to realise that much of the hostile propaganda coming from within and without the Province was just that, propaganda, with little basis in reality.

There were several bombs in Omagh during those years. The town, one never-to-be-forgotten evening, was torched and amongst the victims in High Street were some of our own members. One of them at least, Desmond Black, was burnt out repeatedly, but he rebuilt without recrimination! Such was the character of the Omagh people during those dark days. J B Anderson's and Wm Porter's businesses were bombed and in the event, J B Anderson was never rebuilt. Its Managing Director, John Cathcart, was a member of session.

The times are reflected in a number of tangible memorials dedicated in Trinity during my ministry. These include:

Church Bell   Installed and dedicated "In memory of those who served in the two World Wars and the present struggle in Northern Ireland."

Church Memorial to the Fallen   Unveiled on 10 February 1991.

In addition there were several joint Churches Services for Peace. One was held in the Town Hall, Omagh on 30 September 1972 and a variety of inter church initiatives were undertaken.

So far as the Church was concerned, one could not but feel privileged to be Minister of a congregation with such a noble and honourable history. Occupying the same site for over 200 years, it was like a symbol of hope and faith during the earlier and later 'Troubles'. Attendances were always close on 300 - 350 and the quality of the music steadily improved under the present organist and choir-master. The robing of the choir by Blanche and Fred Todd in 1989 was the final accolade on the lives of two very wonderful parishioners.

Meanwhile during those years the church buildings were not neglected. The church bell, a gift of the Bishop of Clogher and a brother-in-law of the late Mrs Eileen Coote, was installed in 1974 - erected and financed by the ex-servicemen in memory of their comrades in war. The memorial register of those who served in both world wars was brought up to date at a very impressive service in the Church, when the preacher was the Rt Rev Jim Harkness, Chaplin General, N I Command. These are memories that crowd into one's remembrance as the scenario unfolds.

The updating of the memorial record in the Church porch, carried out by Laurence Rushe, is worthy of note. The gilt lettering, set against a background of royal blue perspex, makes it distinctive and easily read. Much of the history of the Church is contained in it.

The extension of the Hall, the refurbishment of the kitchen, the addition of the Games Room, the updating of the Hall heating system, the revival of the BB and GB after some years of lapse - all this is part of the story. The final effort was the complete rebuilding of the church organ and the provision of the elegant new choir chairs, themselves saved from the fire which almost destroyed Church House in Belfast. They were given by Mrs Florence Cathcart in memory of her husband John. The Church building bears the marks of the love of its people and they are to be both congratulated and thanked, now and for the days to come.

The Omagh Bombing 1998

By Rev R Herron

IN May 1993, having served as minister of Strabane Presbyterian Church for the previous eight years, I was installed as minister of Trinity, Omagh and Gillygooley. During my years in Omagh the people of Northern Ireland, with the help of the British and Irish Governments and others beyond these islands, have been trying to find a political solution to those issues which are regarded as the cause of the 'troubles'. The first major sign of progress came in August 1994 when the Provisional IRA declared a complete cessation of violence. Sadly the violence was not over. The following four years were marked by the IRA breaking its ceasefire and bombing Canary Wharf in London and annual disturbances in loyalist and nationalist areas throughout the 'marching season'. In spite of these setbacks the 'peace' process continued and there was a political breakthrough with the signing of the Belfast Agreement on Good Friday, April 1998.

During that year it became clear that not all Irish republicans supported the 'peace process'. Republican 'dissidents' bombed several towns in Northern Ireland.

On Saturday, 15th August 1998, republican terrorists drove a red Vauxhall Cavalier car into Omagh and parked it in Market Street. It was packed with explosives. The telephone warning proved to be misleading and hundreds of people were within a short distance of the bomb when it exploded at 3.10 p.m. The scene was one of bloody devastation. Twenty nine people, including men, women and children, and two unborn children died as a direct result of the bomb. Many people were seriously injured and the traumatic effect has been widespread.

Rev Herron speaking at the Act of Prayerful Reflection, Saturday 22 August, 1998

No members of Trinity were killed in the Omagh bombing but some sustained serious injuries. Members of Trinity have been involved in the aftermath of the tragedy as they have lived out their lives in the local community. The psychological impact of the Omagh bombing is still with us in 2004 and many people have struggled to find a sense of normality.

Sylvia McGrew, a member of Trinity congregation, was seriously injured in the Omagh bombing. She spent ten days in intensive care in the Royal Victoria Hospital with injuries to her legs, abdomen and face. She lost an eye, has perforated eardrums and has a multitude of scars over her body.

On 16th May 1999, the morning service in Trinity was broadcast on Radio Ulster; Sylvia McGrew told her story:

> I don't remember leaving my house on the 15th August. It must have been around 3 o'clock. I only remember coming out of intensive care ten days later and being told what happened to me as well as what happened to others. At first I was totally confused. I could not believe that such an atrocity could happen in our town. I asked myself- "Why me?" - "What did I do to deserve this?" It took a long time for it to sink in.
>
> I have gone through all kinds of emotions. There has been deep sadness and anger. Perhaps being a psychiatric nurse has helped me to cope with some of these emotions. I know it is important to talk about them and try to come to terms with them.
>
> I think I have now reached the stage where I accept what has taken place. The one thing I am very thankful for is that my husband Bill and my three sons were not injured. I don't think I could have coped as well if they had been. I know there are many people worse off than me, including the families of the bereaved and I feel so sorry for them.
>
> I have bad days of course, when I would be thinking about what happened, shedding a few tears for myself and others. Thank God these are getting less.
>
> I had to ask myself, "Am I going to sit back feeling sorry for myself or am I going to push myself on and look to the future?"
>
> So with self-determination and encouragement from Bill and the family, I set myself small goals, like tidying the bed. I had to remind Bill, "I'm doing this myself, don't help". It took a long time to do things, it still does. The first time I vacuumed the hall it took me nearly an hour - but I did it. I just wanted things back to normal, the way they were before the bomb. I wanted my role as wife and mother back.
>
> As well as encouragement from my family, my neighbours, friends and colleagues have kept calling which has been a great help in my recovery. I also received 150 get well cards with prayers enclosed, which showed me that so many people cared for me and were praying for me.
>
> I am able to drive again, after practising on quiet country roads to build up my confidence. Now I drive myself to physiotherapy 3 mornings a week and to the gym for exercise 2 or 3 times per week. This is to build up muscles in both legs.

I keep a diary every day, which I have always done. I can read about my good days and not so good days. One thing I had to do was to go to church. I got out of hospital on 16th September and came to church on Sunday 27th September. It says in my dairy for that day - IT FELT GOOD.

Sadly, like so many others, Sylvia was not able to return to her work because of her injuries.

In Trinity we have attempted to respond to the Omagh bombing in the same way that we try to respond to other tragic events involving human suffering, pain, loss and trouble, with the help of God who is our strength and our salvation.

The Memorial Garden at Drumragh Avenue, Omagh

Small, silent steps

We've looked on darkness -
Those who drove and parked,
Who locked their car and walked away,
Glancing at the faces, as they went;
Catching their reflection, in the glass;
Feeling sunshine's warmth, upon their skin;
Moving, with each step, towards the gloom
Of choices made some little while before
Of what looked good to them and how things should become.

What kind of choices take us to a place like that?
Small, silent steps shape destiny.
And we too place our feet a certain way.
Let us walk where we have light today.

Sheena Herron
19 October 1998 (Jn 12:35)

Postscript

THIS book has attempted to demonstrate how a church, at every age, is totally dependent on its people working together in teams to the glory of God. It has highlighted the Ministers and some of the other people who have given generously of their time and talents to serve this church over its 250 years. The church records prior to 1856 are scant. Consequently the book content has been drawn only from the material available at the time of writing. Whilst huge efforts have been made to provide a comprehensive picture of church life down the years, the authors recognise the selectiveness which has determined the final content. Every attempt has been made to be as accurate as possible and they regret any consequent errors or omissions.

This book has considered the people of Trinity from 1754 to 2004. The photograph below was taken on 11 April 2004. From these young people and their older and younger brothers and sisters will come the officers and decision makers in Trinity Presbyterian Church if it is to move forward to face the challenges and opportunities in the years ahead. These are the people of the future.

Trinity communicants 2004
Back Row (L to R): Dean Pollock, Keith McKnight, Samuel Gallagher (Clerk of Session), Mark Carey.
Middle Row: Alistair Ferguson, Ryan Sommerville, Malcolm Herron, Laura Stronge, Jolene Bell, Lisel Henderson.
Front Row: Rev RWW Clarke (Senior Minister),Chloe McFarland, Johanna Neary, Sara Ferguson, Fiona Dorrian and Rev R Herron.

Appendices

APPENDIX 1

An outline of early Presbyterianism in Ireland

Contributed by Hazel McCay

Up to 1641 Presbyterianism was not a separate entity in Ireland. It was merely a movement within Irish Protestantism. There was one Protestant Church, which had within it two parts- an 'Episcopal' and a 'Presbyterial'. Following the rebellion of 1641 a new ecclesiastical situation emerged. Presbyterianism as a separate entity was established by the formation of the first Presbytery at Carrickfergus on 10 June 1642. For the next 11 years civil wars raged in Ireland and England. Presbyterianism survived both them and Cromwell's attempt to drive out of Ireland all the Presbyterian Ministers and Anglican Bishops.

In 1654 the original Presbytery of Ulster became the Synod of Ulster and was divided into the Presbyteries of Antrim, Down and Route. In 1657 the Presbytery of Laggan was formed out of Route, and in 1659 the Presbytery of Tyrone out of Down. These Presbyteries met in Synod or General Presbytery as and whenever the circumstances of the Church required. During the years 1661-1690 Presbyterianism was suppressed by the state, and times were very difficult. Synod did not meet, and Presbyteries, for the most part, met clandestinely.

From 1690 to 1780 Presbyterians were regarded as second-class citizens, with the denial of their marriages and other legal disabilities. This was the era during which the Second Presbyterian Meeting-house in Omagh was established. Towards the end of the eighteenth century some Presbyterians and some Catholics formed the United Irishmen, seeking to bring together Dissenters, Anglicans and Catholics under a common title. The intention of the movement was to achieve its aims for social reform by constitutional means, but suppression was so intense that the result was the violent rebellion of 1798, which, in turn, was also suppressed with the utmost cruelty. However, the radical strain in Presbyterianism survived the rebellion and, indeed, the domestic difficulties of the first half of the new century when the rural economy collapsed.

The 1859 revival brought about a strengthening of Presbyterianism, which was evangelical and, at that time, increasingly Unionist - a trend that was to continue through the twentieth century and up to the present day.

It is in this historical context that the roots of Presbyterianism in Omagh have developed.

APPENDIX 2

The development of Presbyterianism in Omagh

Contributed by Hazel McCay

This account has been adapted from an article written by Rev W T Latimer, MA, which was published in "The Witness" in 1913:

Historical records dating back to 1670 indicate that Omagh was then only a small village. The hearth money rolls, a kind of taxation, listed just 17 householders liable to pay the tax in question. It may be that a few who were liable were exempt on grounds of poverty. It is thought that Omagh in 1670 could not have contained more than 150 persons. Many farms, which had been left vacant by war and by confiscations, were not taken by colonists from England or Scotland. Considering that the native Irish were Roman Catholics, there were therefore very few Protestants in the Omagh district. The majority of these were Presbyterians, but as their number was small they had at first no stated clergyman.

During the time of Oliver Cromwell's government, salaries were paid to all Protestant clergymen who applied for them and who were known to be 'evangelical', no matter whether they were Presbyterian, Independent, Baptist or Episcopalian.

In 1656 **Robert Brisbane** was a Minister at Drumraw, Termon-McGurk (Clogherney) and 'The Omey' on a salary of £100 a year. Although the reason is unclear, he was ordered to 'remove', and in 1658 it was reported that he had been suspended, but he was afterwards restored. The Protestant denomination to which Brisbane belonged is not known, but it is accepted that he was not Presbyterian, as he was opposed by the Presbytery.

For a number of years Termon-McGurk and Omagh united to form a single congregation, and in 1658 Rev **Robert Wilson**, a firm Presbyterian, succeeded Rev Brisbane. However, he was soon removed to Strabane, from which he was excluded as a Presbyterian, following the restoration of King Charles II.

For some years after 1658 the Omagh Presbyterians were without a regular Minister, but **Mr John Rowatt**, who was in charge of Badoney and Cappagh, occasionally supplied the pulpit and baptised their children.

The era of Mr Rowatt's involvement with Omagh Presbyterianism is hereafter highlighted in some detail. It reflects well the state of Presbyterianism in the town in the period 1660-1690 and gives an interesting insight into the life and times of the people.

Mr Rowatt became caretaker Minister of Drumragh around 1672. Cappagh and Drumragh worshipped in one church and that resulted in the church (at Cappagh) being overcrowded. When approached about this, the Presbytery suggested that the people of Drumragh should build an aisle for themselves in the house at Cappagh. This advice was not followed, and shortly afterwards Clogherney 'successfully' asked to share Mr Rowatt's labours. The basic problem was that there were too many parishes and too few clergy to give appropriate pastoral care or even preach at each church on Sundays.

As a reward for his labours the Drumraw part of Mr Rowatt's congregation was bound to pay him only £5 a year, but even this small amount was not always forthcoming despite regular pressure from the Presbytery. There was little improvement in the next few years, but some wealthy parishioners pledged additional contributions to stipend. These pledges were welcome. It is clear that many Ministers at this time had difficulty in getting even the meagre stipend promised to them, and it was common for some to seek additional income from farming or teaching.

In January 1676, Longfield (Drumquin) asked the Presbytery for a preacher. This was granted and - you have guessed it - Mr John Rowatt was ordered to give them one day in five. This meant that he spent three Lord's Days in Cappagh, a fourth in Clogherney and a fifth in Longfield. This did not take into account Drumraw, but it is presumed that the joint place of meeting for Cappagh and Drumraw previously recommended had been procured somewhere near "The Omey", as had been advised, and it is thought that this house stood in Crevenagh.

The next period saw considerable dissatisfaction among the local Churches, with several petitioning the Presbytery for a greater share of a Minister. A newly arrived Minister, Rev Samuel Halliday, objected to having to officiate in two Meeting-houses. This was resolved, but later Mr Halliday was sent by Presbytery to Connaught on a missionary tour, accompanied by Rev William Henry of Ballyshannon. This was met with great fury and opposition by the Episcopalian Bishop of Killala, Thomas Otway, who was so enraged at the two clergymen's daring attempts to preach the Gospel in his diocese that he had them both put in prison.

While Mr Halliday was away the pulpit was once again occupied by the good old stand-by, Mr Rowatt of Cappagh. But not without drama! On one occasion, when he was baptising a child before the congregation, a magistrate named Eckin ran in furiously to arrest him, but he managed to flee and escape. The reason for this altercation would appear to have stemmed from the Episcopalian Church authorities' prejudices against Presbyterians, when laws dealing with Protestant Nonconformity were enforced more severely than laws against Roman Catholicism. Indeed, for some time Presbyterians, when married by their own clergymen, often ran the risk of imprisonment by an Episcopalian Bishop on a charge of being adulterers. A Presbyterian clergyman was also liable to a fine of £100 by the civil authorities if he was found guilty of dispensing the sacrament of the Lord's Supper. Difficult times indeed!

Mr Halliday eventually left Omagh, preferring an offer of £30 and 20 bushels of corn from Ardstraw to the local offer of a stipend of £33 a year, a house and a farm of land, which the people offered to plough and sow for the first year and to plough in the following years.

In the early 1690s additional Protestant settlers from Scotland and England arrived in the Omagh area. They rented the unoccupied farms, thus increasing both the numbers and the wealth of the area. Consequently the Church could afford to offer a higher stipend. At that time Ministers also received the Royal Bounty, a gift from King William III, which amounted to about £25 a year and was most useful.

APPENDIX 3

Baptisms 1821-1859
In the 1820s the names of families who had their children baptised in Second Omagh were: Alexander, Andrew, Armour, Bell, Brown, Buchanan, Caldwell, Campbell, Carson, Casswell, Cathcart, Charlton, Crawford, Cummings, Cunningham, Dean, Denny, Dunlop, Fair, Glass, Graham, Greer, Gunn, Hamilton, Hanson, Holmes, Houston, Irwin, Kelso, Little, Love, Marshall, Maxwell, McCausland, McConkey, McCrory, McCutcheon, McEldowney, McFarland, McKnight, McPhillomy, Miller, Moorhead, Murdock, Nixon, Orr, Osbrough, Patterson, Peters, Porter, Robb, Rodgers, Smith, Sproule, Surgeon, Wallace, Wason, White, Whyte, Wilson.

In the 1830s the names were: Aiken (or Eakin), Alcorn, Alexander, Armour, Beatty, Booth, Brolly, Buchanan, Burns, Busby, Caldwell, Carson, Casswell, Charlton, Crawford, Denny, Donaghy, Dunlop, Fair, Gardner, Graham, Greer, Hamilton, Harvey, Holmes, Hunter, Irwin, Johnston, Kilpatrick, Kyle, Lindsay, Love, Marshall, Matthews, McClean, McConkey, McCrory, McCutcheon, McEldowney, McElmurray, McFarland, McGaw, McKernaghan, McKinney, McMaster, Miller, Mitchell, Moorhead, Murdock, Orr, Osbrough, Patterson, Porter, Ramsay, Robson, Rodgers, Sharp, Smith, Smyth, Taylor, Wallace, Warnock, Wason, White, Wilson, Wray.

In the 1840s the names were: Alexander, Baxter, Buchanan, Clements, Cuthbertson, Denny, Dudgeon, English, Holmes, Houston, Liggett, Love, Lyons, McAdams, McConkey, McEldowney, McFarland, McKernaghan, Moorhead, Osbrough, Porter, Robinson, Scott, Smith, Smyth, Thompson, White.

In the 1850s the names were: Alexander, Baxter, Carr (or Kerr), Clarke, Dinsmore, Dudgeon, Gibson, Gordon, Hanna, Houston, Lyons, Matthews, McAdams, McCauley, McCullagh, McEldowney, Meeke, Orr, Smyth, Thompson, Todd, White.

Communicants 1825-1828
A list of Communicants for the years 1825 to 1828 was found towards the back of the book. The Minister at this time was Rev David Gilkey. The Communicants were:
1825: Sarah Charleton, Matilda Perry, Lydia McFarland, Mary Barnhill, Margaret Barnhill, John Charleton and David McClean.
1826: Joseph McEldowney, James Orr, Mary Caldwell, Jane Graham, William Graham, Margaret McFarland, William Graham Junior, James Smith, Thomas Graham and Jane McClelland.
1827: William Young, Mary Caldwell, Eleanor McTherazan, Jane Graham, Anne Graham and Rebecca Orr.
1828: William Smith, Alexander Graham, George White, Frances Johnston, Mary Graham and Martha Osbrough.

Marriages 1843
Two marriages were also recorded for the year 1843 by Rev Josias Mitchell:
Matthew Miller and Isabella Osbrough (from Collaghy) on 24 April 1843.
Witnesses:	William Osbrough, Aughaleyne	William Adams, Collaghy
William Graham, Dromore Parish and Anne Thompson, Drumraw, Co Tyrone, on 24 September 1843.
Witnesses:	Father and brother of bride	William White, Fireagh

APPENDIX 4

Second Omagh/Trinity Presbyterian Church, Omagh

List of Elders

SURNAME	FIRST NAME	ADDRESS	OCCUPATION	ORDAINED	ENDED
Andersom	William	Tattynuer, Omagh		Probably 1754	d.
Anderson	Joseph	Market Street, Omagh	Managing Director	Bef 1903	d. 1921
Anderson	M.T.	Donaghanie, Omagh	Rates Collector		d. 1932
Black	Desmond	Kingsbridge, Irishtown, Omagh	Managing Director	10 Jan. 1982	
Campbell	David	Omagh		Probably 1754	d.
Cathcart	Thomas J.	Market Street, Omagh	Managing Director	24-Oct-34	d. 24 Mar1947
Cathcart	John A.	35 Gortmore Gardens, Omagh	Managing Director	15-Apr-56	d. 1981
Coote	Arthur H.	Campsie Road, Omagh	Accountant, Co. Council	24-Oct-34	d. Apr. 1956
Coote	William	Strathroy House, Omagh	Greengrocer	7 Dec. 1975	d. 1999
Crawford	J.	Dublin Road, Omagh	Merchant	17 Jun. 1928	d. 7 Nov 1937
Crawford	Joseph Jun.	33 Dublin Rd. Omagh	Merchant	24 Oct. 1934	d. 1972
Cummins	Mrs Joan	9 Carnoney Road, Omagh	Nursing Auxillary	18 Jun. 1995	
Cuthbertson	Wm. Marshall	Edenvale Park, Omagh	Retired farmer	Co-opt27/5/1987	d. 1997
Cuthbertson	Gladys	Edenvale Park, Omagh	Civil Servant	17 Apr.1988	
Dale	William	John Street, Omagh	Merchant	Bef 1908	d. 1913
Dale	Roberts	24 John Street, Omagh	Merchant	1923	d. 1936
Dickie	Thomas Coulter	Clonavon, Hospital Rd., Omagh	Solicitor	inc 1882	d. 1908
Donald	Noel	Knockgreenan Park, Omagh	Accountant	10 Jan. 1982	
Duffield	Derek	Belvedere Park, Omagh	Accountant, W. E. L. B.	18 Jun. 1995	
Duncan	Albert E.	Gortin Road, Omagh	Farmer	24-Oct-34	d. 23 Aug 1964
Elliott	Robert A.	Townview Ave. Sth., Omagh	Teacher/Administrator	10 Jan. 1982	
Ferguson	Robert	Campsie Road, Omagh	Accountant, Co. Council	inc 1890	d. 1891
Gallagher	Samuel J.	Strathroy, Omagh	Printer	17 Apr.1988	
Gibson	George			inc 1890	d.
Gilmour	Dr Samuel	2 Breezemount Park, Omagh	Doctor	7 Dec. 1975	d. 1979
Graham	S. Charles	Beechgrove, Omagh	Bus driver	10 Jan. 1982	
Greer	James Sen.	Coneywarren, Omagh	Solicitor	bef 1856	d. 1872
Houston	John	Mountjoy, Omagh	Merchant and Auctioneer	bef 1856	d.
Jardine	Colin	11 Corlea Road, Omagh	Valuation Officer	17 Apr.1988	
Johnston	W.H.	47 Dergmoney Heights, Omagh	Policeman	Co-opt 1966	d. 1982
Keys	Ronald	Dromore Road, Omagh	Bank Manager	18 Jun. 1995	
Knox	Samuel J.	Hospital Road, Omagh	Mechanic/engineer	17 Apr. 1988	
Leitch	A.C.	Lovers Retreat, Omagh		1923	d. 1926
Logan	Noel	9 Belvedere Park, Omagh	Bank Manager	Co-opt7/12/1975	left
MacKenzie	Duncan	7 James Street, Omagh	Agriculturalist	15 Apr. 1956	d. 1977
Martin	William	Ardarragh Cottage, Omagh	Finance Officer, Scotts Mill	Co-opt15/4/1956	d. 27 June 1970
McAdam	John	High Street, Omagh	Druggist and Grocer	inc 1879- 1890	d.
McAdam	Thomas J.	Campsie Road. Omagh	Pharmacist	Bef 1890	d. 1945
McCandless	John W.	12 Knocksilla Park, Omagh	Env. Health Officer	10 Jan. 1982	
McCauley	Harold	Arleston, Omagh	Merchant	15-Apr-56	d.1992
McCay	Robert Samuel	86 Drumrawn Road, Drumquin	Farmer	17 Apr. 1988	
McCay	John	Unshinagh, Drumquin	Engineer/Farmer	18 Jun. 1995	
McClure	Norman	50 Dromore Road, Omagh	Headmaster	15 Apr. 1956	d. 1981
McConkey	J.J.	T and F Hospital	Chief Nurse,T & F Hospital	Bef 1928	d. 1943
McFarland	Arthur W.	Dublin Road, Omagh	Draper	24-Oct-34	d. 13 Jan 1964
McFarland	Arthur	74 Dublin Road, Omagh?	Builders Merchant	15-Apr-56	d. 1980
McFarland	Arthur (Artie)	99 Denamona Road, Omagh	Farmer	18 Jun. 1995	
McKnight	Joseph	Campsie Road, Omagh	Woolen draper	bef 1856	d.1860
McKnight	William J	17 Campsie Road	Clerk, Omagh Union	bef. 1856	d. 1898

McMullen	James A.	McClay Park, Omagh	BT engineer	17 Apr. 1988	
Millar	W. Jamie A.	Knockgreenan Park, Omagh	Headmaster	10 Jan. 1982	left 1984
Mitchell	W.S.	13 Edenvale Park, Omagh	Retired farmer	Co-opt7/12/1975	left
Monteith	Robert S.	Dunard, Dublin Road, Omagh	Shoe merchant	24-Oct-34	d. 10 Sept 1969
Moore	Trevor		V.A. T. Officer	Co-opt 1981	left 1981
Moore	John	76 Clanabogan Road, Omagh	Banker/Timber merchant	18 Jun. 1995	
Orr	David G.	Loughmuck, Omagh	Farmer	15-Apr-56	d. 16 Aug 1963
Orr	Ronald	64 Fireagh Road, Omagh	Farmer	7 Dec. 1975	
Porter	William	Grove House, Knocksilla Park	Estate Agent	7 Dec. 1975	d. 1990
Robinson	Thomas J.	5 Gortmore Drive, Omagh	Nursing Home proprietor	15-Apr-56	d. 1990
Rodger	Thomas	Edergole, Omagh		Probably 1754	d.
Scott	John	Strathroy, Omagh		Probably 1754	d.
Scott	William	Gortmore	Superintendent, GNR Railwy.	inc 1890	d.
Stevenson	Ivan	16 Sunnycrest Gardens, Omagh	Dept of Agriculture	Co-opt22/10/1971	left 1973
Swan	Robert Douglas	Ashdene, Omagh	Shoe merchant	Bef. 1903	d. 1932
Thompson	Andrew	25 Cannon Hill, Omagh	Laundary official	7 Dec. 1975	left 1982
Todd	Herbert B.	117 Brookmount Rd., Omagh	Office Manager	15-Apr-56	left 1976
Todd	Frederick	Knockbeg, Lammy, Omagh	Merchant/Farmer	7 Dec. 1975	left 1994 d. 1999
Weir	Edgar J.	Hospital Road, Omagh	Draughtsman	15-Apr-56	Left 1965
White	John J.	Beagh, Omagh	Hardware merchant	Bef 1903	d. 1906
White	George	Loughmuck, Omagh	Merchant	Bef. 1903	d. Jan/Feb 1930
White	James C.	Riverdale, Omagh	Builder	15-Apr-56	d. 1990

Second Omagh/Trinity Presbyterian Church, Omagh

List of Church Committee Members

SURNAME	FIRST NAME	ADDRESS	OCCUPATION	ELECTED	ENDED	REMARKS
Adams	James	4 Dergmoney Heights, Omagh	Retired forestry worker	1995		
Aiken	Andrew A.	Edenvale Park, Omagh	GNR official	1982	died 2002	
Alexander	Samuel	Tamlaght, Omagh	Farmer	inc 1907	1916	d. 1916
Alexander	David			1919	1925	
Allen	Kenneth	Knockgreenan Avenue, Omagh	WELB employee	1990		
Allison	William	Killybrack, Omagh	builder	inc 1907		
Andersom	William	Tattynuer, Omagh		1752		
Anderson	Joseph	Market Street, Omagh	Man. Director, J.B.Anderson 1913-21	inc 1882	ordained elder bef. 1903	d.1921
Anderson	Capt. John B.	Mount Pleasant, Coneywarren	Man. Director, J.B.Anderson 1921-28	1915		d.1928
Anderson	M.T.	Donaghanie, Omagh	Rate Collector	1929	1932	d. 1932
Angus	J	30 Gortmore Gardens, Omagh		1961		
Barr	John	Holmview Terrace, Omagh	Newspaper Editor, Tyrone Constitution	1894	1903	d. 1903
Barr	Mrs	Holmview Terrace, Omagh	Widow of John Barr	1926	1947	d. April 1948
Baxter	Hamilton	Knockgreenan Park	Bank Manager, Ulster Bank	1982		left
Black	Miss	Aughnamoyle, Omagh	Sat in Church with Miss A Buchanan	1926	1932	
Black	R	Glenview Terrace, Omagh	Engineer	1932	1947	
Black	D.	High Street, Omagh	Merchant, Blacks of Omagh	1919	1929	d. 1945
Black	Desmond	Kingsbridge, Irishtown, Omagh	Man. Director, Blacks of Omagh	1965	Ordained elder in 1982	
Booth	George			bef 1856		
Borland	Reginald	3 Gortmore Gardens, Omagh	Bank Manager	1958	again in 1967	left 1970
Brodie	James	Spillars Place	Manager, Gas Works	inc 1907		
Browne	William	10 Lisnahearney Road, Omagh	Farmer	1982	d. 1991	
Buchanan	John	Killyclogher		bef 1856		
Buchanan	John	Bonnynubber		bef 1856		
Buchanan	Miss A.			1926	1927	
Buchanan	Dr. James	Killyclogher, Omagh	Doctor	1942	1943	d. 1943
Burton	A.E.	Hospital Road, Omagh	Grocer	1928	1929	
Burton	Archibald	Clements Villas, Omagh	Grocer	1976	d. 1985	
Campbell	David	Omagh		1752		
Campbell	James	Church Street, Omagh	Insurance agent	1896		
Canning	James	Townview Avenue, Omagh	Bank Manager	1976		left
Carson	J.D.	Edenfel Cottage, Omagh		1929	1948	d. 1948
Carson	Samuel Jun	3 Townview Ave. Sth., Omagh		1995		
Cathcart	Thomas J.	Market Street, Omagh	Man. Director, J.B.Anderson 1928-47	1927	Ordained elder in 1934	d. Mar 1947
Cathcart	John A.	35 Gortmore Gardens, Omagh	Man. Director, J.B.Anderson 1947-1981	1948	Ordained elder in 1956	d.1981
Chambers	A.D.	Ulster Bank, Omagh	Banker, Ulster Bank	1943		left
Chisholm	Robert	17 John Street, Omagh	Blacksmith	1982	d. 1987	
Clarke	Mrs Alice	The Manse, Coneywarren, Omagh	Minister's wife	1985		
Colhoun	William	Mullaghmeena	Farmer	1894	1918	d. 1921
Colhoun	William Jun	Son of Wm. (died 1918)		1919	1922	d.1922
Colhoun	A.F.	Derry Road, Omagh	Solicitor	1934		d. 1982
Colhoun	Norman G.	Mullaghmeena	Farmer	1985		left 2003
Coote	A.H.	Campsie Road, Omagh	Accountant,Clerk to County Council	1928	Ordained elder in 1934	d. Apr 1956
Coote	William	Strathroy House, Omagh	Greengrocer / farmer	1957	Ordained elder 1975	d. 1999
Coulter	Samuel	Lammy	Farmer	1894	inc 1915	
Crawford	Joseph Sen		Jt. Proprietor, Crawford and Crawford	1916	Ordained elder 1923	d. Nov 1937
Crawford	Henry			1919	1927	d. 1927
Crawford	James	Aughnamoyle, Omagh		1934	1939	
Crawford	Joseph Jun.	33 Dublin Road, Omagh	Merchant, Crawford and Crawford	1928	Ordained elder 1934	d. 1972
Cummins	Joan	9 Carnoney Road, Omagh	Nursing Auxillary	1985	Ordained elder 1995	
Cuthbertson	M.	Edenvale Park, Omagh	Retired	1987	Elder co-opted 1987	d. 1997
Cuthbertson	Gladys	Edenvale Park, Omagh	DOE Employee	1985	Ordained elder in 1988	
Dale	William	Crevenagh, Omagh ???	Grocer and Baker	inc 1882	ordained elder abt. 1907	d.1913
Dale	Roberts	John Street, Omagh	Merchant	1914	Ordained elder 1923	d. 1936

Surname	Name	Address	Occupation			
Dick	Thomas	Lisnamallard, Omagh	Auctioneer and Estate Agent	1936	1945	d. 1945
Dick	W.R.	Lisnamallard, Omagh		1937		
Dickie	Thomas C.	Clonavon, Hospital Road, Omagh	Solicitor, 13 High Street, Omagh	inc 1868	ordained elder bef.1882	d. 1908
Dickie	John F.	Clonavon, Hospital Road, Omagh		inc 1912	1920	
Donald	Noel	Knockgreenan Park, Omagh	Accountant	1982	Ordained elder in 1982	
Donnell	Mrs Pearl	12 Edinburgh Park, Omagh		1995		
Dudgeon	William	Ballynahatty		bef 1856		
Duncan	Albert	Gortin Road, Omagh	Farmer	1930	Ordained elder 1934	d. Aug 1964
Dunne	George	Festival Park, Omagh		1988	retired 1998	
Elliott	Neville	Derry Road, Omagh		inc. 1912	1920	
Elliott	Robert A.	Townview Avenue Sth., Omagh	School teacher / administrator	1965	Ordained elder in 1982	
Fallows	John	17 Campsie Road, Omagh	Monumental Sculptor	1885		d. 1902
Fallows	Joseph	8 Campsie Avenue, O magh	Monumental Sculpter / undertaker?	1894	6/11/02	d. 1902
Ferguson	Robert	26 Campsie Road, Omagh	Accountant	inc 1882	Ordained elder bef 1890	d. 1891
Ferguson	Armour J.	Fortlands, Coneywarren	Rates Officer, Tyrone County Council	1885	1927	d. 1929
Fleming	J			1928	1933	
Forsythe	Bertie	Sunnycrest Gardens. Omagh	Agriculturalist	1976		left in
Gallagher	Samuel J.	Strathroy, Omagh	Printer	1985	Ordained elder in 1988	
Gibson	George			bef 1856	ordained elder bef.1890	
Gibson	George Jun.			1890		
Gilmore	Derek	24 Carnoney Road, Omagh		1995		
Gilmour	Dr Samuel	2 Breezemount Park, Omagh	Psychiatrist	1965	Ordained elder 1975	d. 1979
Gilmour	Neil	Breezemount Park, Omagh	Laboratory technician	1982		left 1985
Gordon	John A.	15 McClay Park, Omagh	Dep. Of Agric. Officer	1965		left 1967
Gourly	J.	160 Kevlin Road, Omagh	Joiner	1957		
Graham	J.P	Gortmore, Omagh	Dairy proprietor, Lisbuoy Dairy	1957		d. 1968
Graham	S.Charles	Beechgrove, Omagh	Bus driver	1976	Ordained elder in 1982	
Greer	James Sen.	Coneywarren, Omagh	Solicitor	bef 1856	ordained elder bef. 1856	
Greer	James Jun	19/21 High Street, Omagh	Solicitor	bef 1856		
Greer	Edward	Coolnagarde	Solicitor	bef 1856		
Hall	J.J.	Burnside Villa, Killyclogher	Contractor	1929	1948	d. 1948
Hall	Miss D.	Derry Road, Omagh	School Principal, Corrickbridge	1946		d. 1961
Hamilton	John	Bridge Street, Omagh	Woolen draper	1894	1927	d. 1927
Hamilton	William C.	McClay Park, Omagh	Policeman	1976	d. 2000	
Hamilton	Andrew	Crevenagh Drive, Omagh	Civil Servant	1995		
Houston	John	Mountjoy, Omagh	Auctioneer	bef 1856	ordained elder bef 1856	
Houston	Ross	23 High Street, Omagh	Woolen draper	1885		
Houston	King	Mullaghmore, Omagh	Solicitor	inc 1882	1927	d. 1936
Houston	William	10-12 Georges St. Omagh	Hardware / grocer / Coal / timber merchant	1894		
Hussey	Mrs Caroline	11 Townview Ave. Nth., Omagh	Social worker	1995		
Jardine	Colin	11 Corlea Road, Omagh	Valuation Officer	1985	Ordained elder in 1988	
Johnston	W.G. (Const.)	Clements Villas, Omagh	Policeman	1946	1948	left 1948
Johnston	Dr. J. M.	Stone Bridge, Omagh	Psychiatrist	1949		
Johnston	W.H.	47 Dergmoney Heights, Omagh	Retired policeman	1967	Co-opted elder	d. 1982
Johnston	Thomas J.	Townview Avenue, Omagh	Valuation Oficer	1976	left 1979	
Kennedy	Maurice	35 Sunningdale, Omagh		1967		left
Kerr	John J.	Ballinamullan	Farmer	1885		
Kerr	J.J.	related to John J. (Ballinamullan)		1919	1927	
Keys	Ronald	151 Clanabogan Road, Omagh	Bank Manager	1991	Ordained elder 1995	
Kincaid	James	Pinewood Avenue, Omagh	Electricity Board employee	1976	d. 1991	
Kirk	Hugh	Ashdene, Omagh	Boot and Shoe merchant	1883		d. 1914
Knox	Uel	Hospital Road, Omagh	Operations manager	1985	Ordained elder in 1988	
Leckey	James	Edergole, Omagh	Farmer	1919	1924	
Leitch	A.C.	Lovers Retreat, Omagh		1919	ordained elder 1923	d. 1926
Leitch	Ian	8 Crevenagh Drive, Omagh	Environmental Health Officer	1985		
Logan	Noel	9 Belvedere Park, Omagh	Bank Manager	1975	Elder Co-opted 1975	d. 1994
Lyons	Robert	1 Gortmore Terrace, Omagh		1885	Left for Bangor in1929	d. 1934
Lyons	James	Correnarry, Gortin Road, Omagh	Dentist	inc 1882	1918	d. 1919
Lyons	J.J.		LDS	1928	1933	d. 1934
MacKenzie	Duncan	7 James Street, Omagh	Horticulturalist	1930	Ordained elder in 1956	d. 1977
MacKenzie	Mrs Jean	James Street, Omagh	Public representative	1961		d. 1980
Maginnis	Nathaniel	35 Johnston Park, Omagh	Printer	1985		d. 1993

Maguire	R	Lislimnaghan, Omagh	Coachman to Miss Black	1934	1956	d. 1961
Maguire	R	Johnston Park, Omagh	Painter	1982		
Martin	William	Ardarragh Cottage, Omagh	Accountant, Scotts Mills, Omagh	1956	Co-opted in 1956	d. 1970
Matthews	Samuel	Lisnagir, Cappagh		bef 1856		
Mawhinney	Hugh			1919		
Maxwell	J.W.			1752		
McAdam	John	High Street, Omagh	Druggist and grocer	bef 1856	ordained elder bef 1856	
McAdam	T.J.	32 Campsie Road, Omagh	Pharmacist, McAdam and Bates	1885	ordained elder abt 1888	d. 1948
McAdam	R.W.	43 High Street, Omagh	Chemist	1894	1920	d. 1920
McAdam	Miss N.	3 Townview Avenue, Omagh	School Principal, Cavanacaw	1949		
McAuley	Josias		brother of Harold McCauley	1919	1927	d. 1927
McCandless	John W.	12 Knocksilla Park, Omagh	Environmental Health Officer	1976	Ordained elder in 1982	
McCarthy	John			bef 1856		
McCauley	Harold	Arleston, Old Mountfield Road,Omagh	Entrepreneur/farmer	1928	Ordained elder in 1956	d.1992
McCay	Robert S.	86 Drumrawn Road, Drumquin	Farmer	1982	Ordained elder in1988	
McCay	John	Unshinagh, Drumquin	Engineer/Farmer	1990	Ordained elder 1995	
McClelland	W.J.	Railway Terrace, Omagh	Shop manager	1896		
McCloskey	F		Shop assistant, Bloomfields	1938		
McClure	Norman	50 Dromore Road, Omagh	Headmaster, Campsie Primary	1936	Ordained elder in 1956	d. 1981
McConkey	J.J.		Nursing Officer, T and F Hospital	1919	Ordained elder bef 1923	d. 1943
McConnell	Robert	1 McConnell Place, Omagh	Proprietor, Stewart Arms Hotel	1885	d. 10 December 1904	d. 1904
McConnell	John Knox	Ashfield House, Tamlaght Rd., Omagh	Solicitor	1894	1934	d. 1935
McConnell	Samuel D.	Edenderry, Omagh	Proprietor/ Electrician	1976	left	
McConnell	Kenneth	Birchwood, Omagh	NIE	1988	retired 1995	
McCorkell	William J.			1885		
McCutcheon	James	34 Edenfel Park, Omagh		1995		
McDermott	Ronald	40 Knockgreenan Park, Omagh	Benefits superintendent	1967		left
McElhinney	Claire	Clanabogan Road, Omagh	Retail grocer	1995		
McElmurray	Andrew			bef 1856		
McElwaine	D.		Civil Servant	1995	left for Gillygooley 1998	
McFadden	Henry	Campsie, Omagh		inc 1896	inc 1897	
McFarland	Arthur W.	Windsor, Dublin Road, Omagh		1939	Ordained elder 1934	d. Jan 1964
McFarland	Arthur	Windsor, 74 Dublin Rd., Omagh	Builders merchant	1950	Ordained elder in 1956	d.1980
McFarland	John	Windsor, Dublin Road, Omagh	Engineer	1965		left 1969
McFarland	Mrs May	Windsor, Dublin Rd., Omagh	Housewife	1976	d. 1984	
McFarland	Artie	99 Denamona Road, Omagh	Farmer	1982	Ordained elder in 1995	
McFarlane	Wm. J.	Market Street, Omagh	Grocer	1900	1927	d. 1927
McGalliard	W.			1936	1937	
McGrew	William J.	Gardenville Avenue	Post Office official	1976	retired 2001	
McKeeman	W.A.	McClay Park, Omagh	Accountant for County Council	1970	left Omagh in1975	
McKnight	Joseph	Campsie Road, Omagh		bef 1856	ordained elder bef. 1856	d. 1860
McKnight	William J.	32 Campsie Road, Omagh	Clerk. Omagh Union	bef 1856	ordained elder bef. 1856	d. 1898
McMullen	James A.	McClay Park, Omagh	BT engineer	1982	Ordained elder 1988	left
McMurray	W.T.		Farmer	1919	1922	
Millar	W.J.			inc 1912	1920	d. 1920
Millar	W.J.A.	Knockgreenan Avenue, Omagh	Schoolteacher	1971	Ordained elder in 1982	left 1984
Milligan	Gary	15 Crevenagh Way, Omagh	Electrical engineer	1995		
Mitchell	Robert	9 Campsie Road, Omagh	Partner, Messrs. Swan and Mitchell	1928		d. 1958
Mitchell	W.S.	13 Edenvale Park, Omagh	Retired farmer	1975	Elder Co-opted 1975	left
Monteith	Robert	Coneywarren, Omagh	Butler	1902	1912	d. 1912
Monteith	Robert S.	Dublin Road, Omagh	Merchant, Swan and Mitchell	1927	Ordained elder in 1934	d. Sept. 1969
Monteith	Raymond	4 Anderson Gardens, Omagh	Plumber	1995		
Moore	W.J. DFC	Dunard, Omagh		1946	1949	
Moore	Herbert H.	Kevlin Road, Omagh	Dept. of Agriculture official	1957		
Moore	Trevor	42 Georgian Villas, Omagh	Valuation Officer	1981	Elder co-opted	left
Moore	John	76 Clanabogan Road, Omagh	Director, Fortress Systems	1990	Ordained elder 1995	
Mullin	George	40 Old Mountfield Road, Omagh	Accountant, Omagh District Council	1982	d.1992	
Nixon	John			1752		
Orr	David G.	Loughmuck, Omagh	Farmer	1956	Ordained elder 1956	d. 1963
Orr	Ronald	64 Fireagh Road, Omagh	Farmer	1965	Ordained elder 1975	
Parke	R. A.	Dublin Road, Omagh	Editor, Tyrone Constitution	1938	retired 1958	d 1974
Parke	Robert	Dublin Road, Omagh	Solicitor, Clerk to Tyrone County Council	1945		d.1993

Surname	Forename	Address	Occupation			
Parke	Gregory	Dublin Road, Omagh	Solicitor	1991		
Patton	Robert			1885		
Perkins	Samuel	Bankmore Road, Omagh	Architect	1985		d. 1997
Porter	William	17 Knocksilla Park, Omagh	Estate Agent and auctioneer	1957	Ordained elder 1975	d. 1990
Porter	Alan	Knocksilla Park, Omagh	Estate Agent and auctioneer	1991		
Preston	J	5 Cannon Dale, Omagh	Choir Leader	1957		
Reid	Andrew			1885		
Robinson	T.J.	5 Gortmore Drive, Omagh	Nursing Home proprietor	1948	Ordained elder in 1956	d. 1990
Rodger	Thomas	Edergole, Omagh		1752		
Ross	D.A.	T and F Hospital	Laundaryman	1913	1927	d. 1927
Roulston	W.J.	Campsie Avenue, Omagh	Shop assistant	1894	inc 1907	
Rule	William			1927	1930	
Rutherdale	J	Oaklands, Omagh	Farmer	1935	1946	left 1947
Rutherdale	Mrs	Oaklands, Omagh			co-opted1944	left 1947
Sayers	Alfred	1 Millbank Court, Omagh	Electrician	1995		
Scott	John	Strathroy, Omagh		1752		
Scott	James			bef 1856		
Scott	William	Gortmore, Omagh	Superintendent, GNR Railway	Bef 1890	ordained elderbef. 1890	
Scott	William			inc 1882		
Simpson	R.A. MA	Dergmoney Place, Omagh	Headmaster, Omagh Academy	1942		d. 1970
Small	Capt. A.			1942	1949	
Smith	William Jun	Gillygooley	farmer	1885		
Sproull	Andrew	High Street, Omagh	Manager, Provincial Bank	1901	1924	d. 1924
Stevenson	Ivan	16 Sunnycrest Gardens, Omagh	Dept. of Agriculture.	1971	Co-opted elder	left 1973
Stewart	Robinson A.	Hospital Road, Omagh	Retired ??	1982	d. 2000	
Stuart	James	Balfour Villa, Omagh	Law clerk	inc 1907	1915	
Swan	Robert D.	Ashdene, Omagh	Shoe Merchant, Swan and Mitchell	1893	ordained elder bef 1903	d. Jan 1932
Thompson	Andrew	25 Cannon Hill, Omagh	Ever Ready salesman	1967	Ordained elder 1975	left 1982
Todd	Herbert B.	117 Brookmount Road,Lammy,Omagh	Office Manager	1936	Ordained elder in 1956	left 1976
Todd	G.F.	Knockbeg, Lammy, Omagh	Merchant, John Stret, Omagh	1957	Ordained elder 1975	d. 1999
Wallace	John A.	15 Gortmore Gardens, Omagh	Agriculturalist	1961		
Warnock	William			bef 1856		
Watson	James	Culmore, Omagh	farmer	1885		
Weir	Edgar	Hospital Road, Omagh	College lecturer / Builder /Draughtsman	1950	Ordained elder in 1956	Left 1965
White	George Jun.	Loughmuck, Omagh	Merchant	1895		d. 1930
White	George	High Street, Omagh	Merchant	Bef. 1903		d. 1930
White	John	28 Market Street, Omagh	Hardware merchant	inc 1895		
White	John J.	Beagh, Omagh	farmer	1890	Ordained elder bef. 1903	d. 1906
White	John	28 Market Street, Omagh	Merchant	inc 1907	1912	d. 1912
White	G.C.	Moorelough		1957	1958	d. 1958
White	G.C.	Dublin Road, Omagh	Merchant, Fishing Tackle	1934		
White	James			1913	1927	
White	J.C.	Riverdale, Omagh	Builder	1946	Ordained elder in 1956	d. 1990
Wilson	James	James Street, Omagh		1894		
Wilson	Joseph	Glenalt, Dublin Road	Man. Director, Crawford and Wilson	1900		d. 1954

Acknowledgments

The authors gratefully acknowledge the contributions of many other people (listed below) in putting together the information assembled in this publication. Particular appreciation is paid to the two local newspapers, the Tyrone Constitution and the Ulster Herald whose publications have been a rich and invaluable source of local history information and reference. Tribute is also paid to the WELB Library Service that has preserved this and much more local information making it easily accessible for present research.

Maureen Archibald
TS Birrell
John Bradley
Patrick Brogan (WELBLS)
Billy Campbell
Ronnie Campbell
Mrs Florence Cathcart
Rev R.W.W. and Mrs Clarke
Audrey Clements
Noel Donald
Jean Faux
Karen Fitzsimmons (WELBLS)
Samuel Gallagher
Ian Giboney
Alan Gibson
Neil Gilmour
David Haddow

Adrian Hamilton
Campbell Henderson
Audrey Hodge
Jack Johnston
Philip McCandless
W.J. McGrew
Rev John McKee
Angus Mitchell
Dr Haldane Mitchell
Rev JF Murdoch
Anne Monteith
Mrs Olive Parke
Mrs Mary Pinkerton
Miss Jean Rea
Jackie Sloan
Joyce Smyth
Herbert B. Todd
Ed. Winters

Presbyterian Historical Society
WELB Library Service (WELBLS)
The Ulster American Folk Park - Centre for Migration Studies
The Ulster Folk and Transport Museum
Images of Omagh
Tyrone Constitution
Ulster Herald

SPONSORS
Fortress Systems
Omagh District Council
Ulster Local History Trust

Index